A HANDBOOK FOR TEACHERS

Effective Instructional Strategies for Content Area Writing

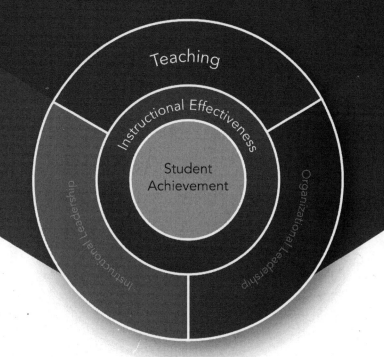

Teaching

Instructional Effectiveness

Student
Achievement

Instructional Leadership

Organizational Leadership

International Center for
Leadership in Education

RIGOROUS LEARNING FOR ALL STUDENTS

Acknowledgment

The International Center for Leadership in Education would like to thank Bernadette Lambert for her contributions to this handbook.

Published by International Center for Leadership in Education, Inc.

Printed in the U.S.A.

ISBN-13: 978-1-935300-96-0
ISBN-10: 1-935300-96-2

International Center for Leadership in Education, Inc.
1587 Route 146
Rexford, New York 12148
(518) 399-2776
fax (518) 399-7607
www.LeaderEd.com
info@LeaderEd.com

Contents

 # Overview

The Daggett System for Effective Instruction

The Daggett System for Effective Instruction (DSEI) provides a coherent focus across the entire education organization on the development and support of instructional effectiveness to improve student achievement. Whereas traditional teaching frameworks are teacher-focused and consider what teachers should do to deliver instruction, DSEI is student-focused and considers what the entire educational system should do to facilitate learning. It is a subtle but important difference based on current research and understanding about teaching and learning.

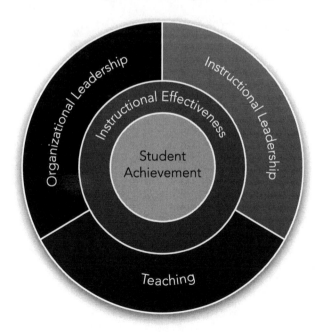

The three parts of DSEI are illustrated here. The following are the critical functions of each part of the system. Think about where you, as a professional educator, fit into this system.

Six Elements of Organizational Leadership

- Create a culture of high expectations.
- Create a shared vision.
- Build leadership capacity.
- Align organizational structures and systems to vision.
- Align teacher/administrator selection, support, and evaluation.
- Support decision making with data systems.

Five Elements of Instructional Leadership

- Use research to establish urgency for higher expectations.
- Align curriculum to standards.
- Integrate literacy and math across all content areas.
- Facilitate data-driven decision making to inform instruction.
- Provide opportunities for focused professional collaboration and growth.

Six Elements of Teaching

- Embrace rigorous and relevant expectations for all students.
- Build strong relationships with students.
- Possess depth of content knowledge and make it relevant to students.
- Facilitate rigorous and relevant instruction based on how students learn.
- Demonstrate expertise in use of instructional strategies, technology, and best practices.
- Use assessments to guide and differentiate instruction.

When all parts of the system are working together efficiently, teachers receive the support they need, and students are successfully prepared for college, careers, and citizenship.

DSEI and Effective Instructional Strategies for Content-Area Writing

The focus of this handbook is on sharing literacy strategies that will significantly help students comprehend, enjoy, and fulfill their writing assignments. The handbook provides ideas on how to use these strategies in all curriculum areas, not just English class. From middle school through high school, the entire school must participate in the effort to raise student levels of literacy.

Introduction

The Introduction suggests a variety of ways a school can implement a successful literacy initiative.

Strategies

The handbook provides a series of strategies that teachers in all curriculum areas can use to raise students' understanding and enjoyment of their writing assignments, from textbooks to nonfiction articles to literary classics. Teachers are provided with step-by-step instructions for Modeling, Guided Practice, and Independent Practice. Strategies come with sample readings and graphic organizers, both blanks that teachers can use as masters and completed versions showing how the organizer is to be filled in.

Using highly effective literacy strategies is a central goal of any district-wide or schoolwide literacy initiative, and for good reason. The choice of strategies can have a significant impact on test scores and student achievement. This handbook describes a number of effective writing strategies and provides structured activities you can use to teach them to your students. It also includes a section that will help you take your students through the five stages of the writing process.

Any good initiative, however, involves more than strategies. While practices and ideas both big and small can change the very culture of a building or district, the classroom is still always the central focus. Therefore, it is important to consider how a literacy initiative fits within a school or district's other initiatives, how it will work within the school or district's culture, and what can be done to enhance what is happening in the classroom.

For example, if a school or district places a strong emphasis on writing as an everyday activity, both for assignments and for pleasure, students get into the habit of self-expression through writing. Consequently, their grammar, usage, and spelling will improve, and they will become more articulate and more highly verbal. This improvement in writing will, in turn, enable students to hone and refine a skill they will use every day of their personal, academic, and future professional lives. What's more, good writing will naturally lead to an improvement in other, related skills—reading, speaking, listening, and reasoning. This handbook provides models and ideas for teaching, developing, and sustaining the skills needed for writing in all content areas.

As you explore the strategies in this handbook, consider your school's literacy level with the following questions:

- Do your writing test scores indicate a sweeping need for change and improvement, or only minor adjustments?

- How much writing is required on tests in content areas other than English (science, math, and so on)? Do those scores indicate that while students may understand the content, they struggle with the type and amount of writing needed to demonstrate proficiency?

© International Center for Leadership in Education

- Do these test scores indicate that students struggle with the type and amount of writing required?

- What is your school doing to address Common Core State Standards in writing?

- Which teachers, coaches, and/or administrators are already experienced in teaching writing across the curriculum?

- How much professional development time does the school or district offer for writing instruction?

 # Introduction

Common Core State Standards: Writing

The purpose of all writing is to communicate. Without the ability to write fluently, swiftly, and articulately, students will not be able to communicate information, thoughts, or ideas effectively, either in school or in the adult world. The Common Core State Standards address this concern by establishing clear goals and expectations in writing and research. There are Common Core State Standards at every grade level from K to 12; there is also a set of College and Career Readiness Standards that teachers can use to measure students' preparedness for graduation through the middle school and high school grades.

The Common Core State Standards in Writing are divided into four categories:

1. **Text Types and Purposes** address the reasons for writing and the different genres in which students are expected to write. "Because it was assigned" is not a sufficient reason for writing. Students must understand that a person writes primarily to communicate, and that there are different types of communication. CCSS identifies three broad categories of writing purposes:

    *   argumentative writing, which supports claims with specific evidence

    *   informative/explanatory writing, which analyzes and conveys information

    *   narrative writing, which describes real or imagined experiences

    These are broad types of writing which include a variety of genres, including research reports, editorials, essays, speeches, prose fiction, poetry, instructions, biography, reviews, and so on.

2. **Production and Distribution of Writing** addresses the writing process, with its five steps of Prewriting, Drafting, Editing, Revising, and Publishing. The standards establish expectations of clarity, coherence, appropriateness of style and subject to audience and task, and use of technology for publication.

3. **Research to Build and Present Knowledge** focuses on gathering the facts and information students will need for many kinds of writing, including finding background information for original fiction, poetry, and drama. Students are expected to conduct appropriate research, gather relevant information, assess the reliability of their sources, and avoid plagiarism. Assessing reliability of sources is a very sophisticated skill associated with Quadrant D instruction in the Rigor/Relevance Framework.

4. **Range of Writing** establishes the expectation that students will write habitually and in a variety of formats. Long-term writing assignments may require research, reflection, and revision. Students must also master the skill of timed writing, which requires a focused approach, concise phrasing, and sticking to the central point.

Teachers should keep these standards in mind as they plan writing assignments for their classes. These standards apply equally well to all curriculum areas. For example, science and history classes require students to do background research, ascertain facts, weigh evidence, and defend their points of view. In the larger world outside of school, the ability to write well and cogently is perhaps second only to the ability to read easily and with comprehension.

Jensen Beach High School: Writing Across the Curriculum

The motto of Jensen Beach High School is "Challenging Every Child to Dream, Aspire, and Achieve," and that is exactly what it has done. Jensen Beach believes in a holistic approach to learning. This approach establishes literacy as one of several priorities that are centered on rigor, relevance, and relationships, and it also includes, among other priorities, 9th grade transition and professional development. The literacy coach at Jensen

Beach is responsible for several schoolwide initiatives, all of which were made possible by the administration's strong commitment to literacy.

As a part of its literacy initiative, which has contributed greatly to the school's overall success, Jensen Beach implemented a schoolwide writing program focused on state and national writing assessments. Using a common rubric, teachers were taught to read essays with an eye toward assessment and were trained on assessment techniques, too. While the literacy coach provided writing prompts when necessary, most departments found and/or created their own writing prompts in their own content areas. To keep assessment consistent, all teachers used the Florida Comprehensive Assessment Test (FCAT) writing rubrics, and all essay assessments counted as quiz scores.

With the help of their literacy initiative, Jensen Beach was able to enhance their students' communication skills and increase the relevance of their curriculum across all content areas. Citing a report from *Business Week*, they underscored how important it will be for students entering the 21st-century economy to communicate quickly and effectively in ways that fluidly cross traditional content-area boundaries. According to the article cited, with the rapid pace at which companies and products are being created almost overnight, any company hoping to maintain its competitive edge must communicate its plan for success to its employees cogently, succinctly, and rapidly. With the help of their holistic model, Jensen Beach integrated all its content areas and were able to choose a set of key topics pertaining to each subject area.

Here's how they integrate literacy across content areas. Every Wednesday from September to May, all students respond to an expository or persuasive writing prompt in a specific subject area. The prompts require students to write at least two single-spaced pages in longhand in 45 minutes. The rotating schedule of content areas is as follows:

- First Wednesday: math
- Second Wednesday: science and physical education
- Third Wednesday: English language arts, social studies, and foreign language
- Fourth Wednesday: CTE, arts, and ROTC

For each subject area, sample prompts follow:

Math

- Describe different ways we use fractions, both in mathematics and in everyday life.
- Describe various ways that performing artists (musicians, actors, dancers, circus performers, etc.) use math on the job.

Science

- Explain how science affects one of the following activities: eating habits, leisure activities, or shopping patterns.
- Explain the physics involved in a piece of playground equipment.

Physical Education

- How can training improve your fitness or your performance in your sport?
- Persuade a friend who claims to hate athletics to try a game or sport you think he or she would enjoy.

English Language Arts

- Decide on an alternative ending to a novel or short story you recently read, either in or outside of class. Explain why you would change the author's original ending, and defend your own idea.
- Who is your favorite author? Why is he or she your favorite? Remember to provide specific details from the author's work to support your answer.

Social Studies—U.S. History

- Explore the causes of the Great Depression.
- Choose a position on the beginnings of U.S. involvement in Vietnam from 1954 to 1960, and then write a letter to the editor of your local newspaper that supports your position. Be sure to provide substantial factual evidence.

Social Studies—Geography

- Compare and contrast human and physical geography. Make sure you give examples of both.

- Describe how geographers have made it possible to locate places on Earth accurately.

Fine Arts and Performing Arts

- Persuade your readers that the arts are as essential to education as reading and math. Use specific evidence to support your argument.

- Choose a musician or group you admire (in any genre of music, from any time period) and explain why you admire him, her, or it. Explain what this musician or group contributes to society through music.

CTE, ROTC

- Consider the following quotation. Take a position, then plan and write an essay persuading readers to support your position.
  - "The dictionary is the only place where success comes before work. Hard work is the price we must pay for success. I think you can accomplish almost anything if you're willing to pay the price." —Vince Lombardi

- Consider the following quotation. Then plan and write an essay that explains your response.
  - "I never did a day's work in my life — it was all fun." — Thomas Edison

While not everyone was comfortable implementing the writing initiative into their courses, Jensen Beach worked very hard to help all teachers. Teachers utilized administrative periods learning how to use the FCAT Writes rubric to grade their students' essays. During the training, teachers had an opportunity to grade sample essays. Posters of the rubric were subsequently displayed in every classroom.

Some students asked: "This isn't English class; why do we have to write?" This question gave teachers a useful opportunity to explain why writing is important to all content areas. Today, both students and teachers at Jensen Beach understand and are comfortable with the process. Once a month, teachers create a prompt that is specific to the content they are presently teaching.

Because all content areas in the curriculum are included in the process, students learn that writing is valued across the school. Teachers, too, realize that everyone can find a way to contribute to, and participate in, a literacy initiative.

While writing across the curriculum is just one part of Jensen Beach's comprehensive literacy plan, it is a crucial element for several reasons:

- Writing is a way for everyone in the school to participate and feel a part of the initiative.
- Writing across the curriculum means everyone is helping to raise FCAT scores, even if a teacher does not teach a core class.
- Asking departments to create writing prompts and assess writing using a common rubric creates a tangible method to measure accountability. Because teachers were required to turn in writing samples to their department chairs and document essay scores in their grade books, they were motivated to "get on board our bus," as Principal Ginger Featherstone put it.
- As teachers became more comfortable with writing, they demonstrated to students that writing is important and, furthermore, that learning new skills is a part of every job. They truly taught by example.

Skill Development for All Students

Suggestions for Working with English Language Learners (ELLs) and Students with Disabilities

When working with English language learners (or culturally and linguistically diverse students) and students with disabilities in a regular education classroom, consider these tips:

- **Model the strategies.** While modeling helps all students, it is essential for ELLs and students with disabilities. Most students can use graphic organizers to learn content more effectively, but graphic organizers pose difficult challenges for ELLs and students with disabilities. Before initiating guided or independent practice of the strategies in this handbook, set the stage for success by first explaining the purpose of using the strategy and then delivering the directions. Once you have done that, model for students how to implement what you explained.

- **Lower the affective filter, or "fear factor."** Having to read their own original writing aloud to the class often creates a great deal of stress for ELL students. Support students by allowing them to work with peers or trained student tutors (often also bilingual) in a comfortable and friendly one-on-one environment. Do not ask students to perform a "cold" reading aloud in class. Instead, allow them to work with partners.

As you work with ELL students and students in special education programs, consider other resources as well, such as *Supporting English Language Learners Systemwide* and *Reinventing Special Education — K12*. Both of these handbooks offer research-based advice for helping all students to succeed.

Peer Tutoring

Having a peer role model—or being asked to become a peer role model—can help integrate high school students into their environment, engage them throughout their high school years, and motivate them to stay in school. Consider supplementing classroom instruction with multi-age peer tutoring, which, when properly implemented, has been shown to produce one of the most powerful results of any intervention.

Assign each 9th grader to work with a struggling middle school student, and also pair him or her with an 11th- or 12th-grade mentor. Mentors can reinforce writing strategies and set an example of positive behavior. Thus all participating 9th graders receive academic and social benefits in both capacities, as mentor and as mentee. Students receive the academic benefits that come from practicing writing skills with a middle school pupil, plus the social and emotional benefits that grow out of a long-term relationship with an older, more motivated mentor.

To the Teacher

Teaching is a craft practiced by skilled professionals, not an exact science in which any person can follow a standard recipe that guarantees success. Even the best teaching recommendations don't work in every situation for every student. Successful teachers not only teach well, but are able to make good decisions about what strategies work in various situations. Successful teachers also learn through experience what works in various instructional activities.

Instead of relying solely on trial and error, this handbook provides a resource for continuous improvement of your craft. The summary of instructional strategies helps you add to your professional "toolkit."

This resource also helps you analyze the variables in teaching situations and systematically select strategies that are likely to lead students to success. When you are comfortable and confident with several instructional strategies, you have choices in creating effective learning experiences. This gives you a much greater chance of presenting a lesson that reaches your students.

As you continue on your journey as a teacher, the suggestions in this handbook will help you to strengthen your professional repertoire and make good decisions about how to present material. Better decisions will lead to more motivated and engaged students. Those satisfying moments when everything works well in teaching are why most teachers joined the profession. Use the ideas in this handbook to increase your effectiveness with students.

Several important concepts are presented in this Introduction that apply to all instructional strategies. The first is the Rigor/Relevance Framework®, a tool developed by the International Center for Leadership in Education to measure the rigor and relevance of curriculum, instruction, and assessment. When you become familiar with the framework, you will be able to use it to facilitate learning experiences for your students that are high in cognitive skill development and contain real-world applications.

Next comes the International Center's Performance Planning Model. The interrelationship of curriculum, instruction, and assessment will become more apparent to you as you explore the complex process of curriculum planning. As a part of this process, instructional strategies can motivate the learner to engage in more rigorous and relevant learning.

Using the Rigor/Relevance Framework

The Rigor/Relevance Framework is a tool developed by the International Center to examine curriculum, instruction, and assessment. It uses a familiar knowledge taxonomy, while encouraging a move to application of knowledge. The Rigor/Relevance Framework helps make explicit the relevance of learning to the real world, broadening the historically narrow focus on acquisition of knowledge.

The Rigor/Relevance Framework is based on two dimensions of higher standards and student achievement. One is a continuum of knowledge based on the six levels of Bloom's Taxonomy, which describes the increasingly complex ways in which we think. The low end is acquiring knowledge and being able to recall or locate that knowledge in a simple manner (acquisition level). Just as a computer conducts a word search in a word processing program, a competent person at this level can scan through thousands of bits of information in the brain to locate that desired knowledge.

Rigor/Relevance Framework®

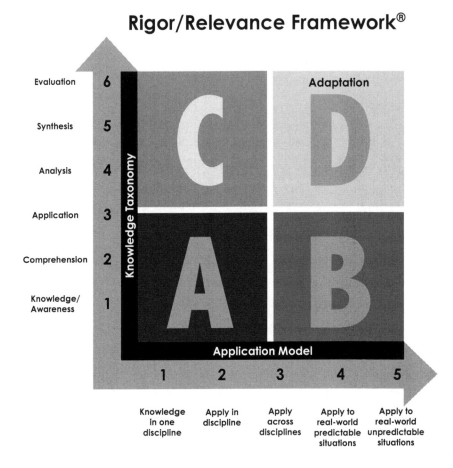

The high end of the knowledge continuum labels more complex ways in which we use knowledge. At this level, knowledge is fully integrated into our minds, and we can do much more than locate knowledge. We can take several pieces of knowledge and combine them in both logical and creative ways. Assimilation of knowledge is a good way to describe this high level of the thinking continuum. Assimilation is often referred to as a higher-order thinking skill. At this level, the student can find effective solutions to complex problems and create unique work.

The other continuum is one of action. While the knowledge continuum can be passive, the action continuum, based on the five levels of the Application Model, describes putting knowledge to use. At the low end (acquisition level), there is knowledge acquired for its own sake. At the high end of the continuum is using that knowledge to solve unpredictable problems, particularly from the real world, and to create projects, designs, and other works.

Together, the Knowledge Taxonomy and Application Model form the Rigor/Relevance Framework. A more extensive discussion of the Rigor/Relevance Framework can be found in *Using Rigor and Relevance to Create Effective Instruction,* published by the International Center. This handbook also includes activities for understanding how to use the framework in planning curriculum and assessment.

The Rigor/Relevance Framework has four quadrants. Quadrant A represents simple recall and basic understanding of knowledge for its own sake. Directly above is Quadrant C, which represents more complex thinking, but still knowledge for its own sake. Examples of Quadrant A knowledge are knowing that the world is round and that Shakespeare wrote *Hamlet.* Quadrant C embraces higher levels of knowledge, such as knowing how the U.S. political system works and analyzing the benefits and challenges of the cultural diversity of this nation versus other nations.

Quadrants B and D represent action or high degrees of application. Quadrant B would include knowing how to use math skills to make purchases and count change. The ability to access information in wide-area network systems and gather knowledge from a variety of sources to solve a complex problem in the workplace is an example of Quadrant D knowledge.

These examples are skills in technical reading and writing.

- **Quadrant A:** Define vocabulary terms needed to understand content of a classroom simulation.
- **Quadrant B:** Complete a simulation following the directions given by the instructor.

- **Quadrant C:** Compare and contrast the information gained from two simulations with that gained from reading a text on the same topic.
- **Quadrant D:** Synthesize information from a range of sources (e.g., texts, media sources, simulations), presenting solutions to conflicting information.

Each of these four quadrants can be labeled with a term that characterizes the learning or student performance that occurs there.

Quadrant A—Acquisition

Students gather and store bits of knowledge and information. Students are primarily expected to remember or understand this acquired knowledge.

Quadrant B—Application

Students use acquired knowledge to solve problems, design solutions, and complete work. The highest level of application is to apply appropriate knowledge to new and unpredictable situations.

Quadrant C—Assimilation

Students extend and refine their knowledge so that they can use it automatically and routinely to analyze and solve problems and create solutions.

Quadrant D—Adaptation

Students have the competence to think in complex ways and also to apply knowledge and skills they have acquired. Even when confronted with perplexing unknowns, students are able to use their extensive knowledge base and skills to create unique solutions and take action that further develops their skills and knowledge.

In 2001 Bloom's Knowledge Taxonomy was updated and revised by Lorin Anderson, a student of Bloom's, and David Krathwohl, a colleague, to reflect the movement to standards-based curricula and assessment. Nouns in Bloom's original model were changed to verb forms (for example, *knowledge* to *remembering* and *comprehension* to *understanding*) and slightly reordered. We believe that the original Bloom's taxonomy as shown in our Rigor/Relevance Framework clearly describes expectations for Quadrants A, B, C, and D. The revised Bloom's elevates the importance of Quadrants B and D and indicates how 21st-century lessons should be built. We regard both the original and revised taxonomies as necessary and important.

The Rigor/Relevance Framework is easy to understand. With its simple, straightforward structure, it can serve as a bridge between school and the community. It offers a common language with which to express the notion of more rigorous and relevant standards and encompasses much of what parents, business leaders, and community members want students to learn.

The framework is versatile; you can use it in the development of instruction and assessment. Likewise, you can use it to measure your progress in adding rigor and relevance to instruction and to select appropriate instructional strategies to meet learner needs and higher achievement goals.

Planning Instruction

To attain higher levels of rigor and relevance, instruction and assessment must not be separate and linear, but rather interrelated. Good learning takes place when there is a dynamic linkage of all components. In rigorous and relevant learning, instruction and assessment should have significant overlap. Authentic assessment should occur naturally as part of the instructional process. The current assessment reform movement seeks to place greater emphasis on student performance as opposed to simply recall of facts. Planning good instruction and assessment is easier if you abandon the image of linear progression of assessment following instruction.

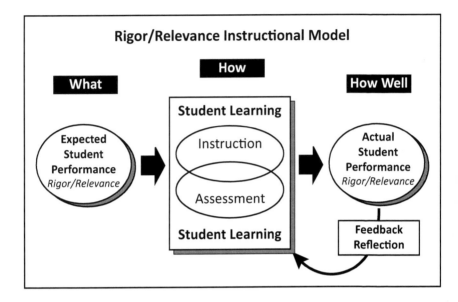

Without effective planning, there is little likelihood that students will achieve the expected rigorous and relevant learning. Curriculum planning is a complex process. It is much more than picking out a work of literature or a textbook chapter and deciding that it would make a good instructional topic. Teacher experience and student data should be considered in order to make thoughtful decisions about instruction and assessment.

When teachers hear the word "curriculum," they generally think of unit or lesson plans that describe teaching procedures and/or student activities that take place in a classroom. It is natural to think about these plans and immediately imagine what they would look like in classrooms. Teachers are under constant pressure to present activities that engage students, and there is little time to do much planning—such is the structure of the U.S. education system.

While curriculum must be organized into unit plans and lessons plans, curriculum planning does not begin with them. Teachers who begin and end their curriculum planning by writing a lesson plan miss important curriculum decisions.

The curriculum is a means to an end: a performance by the student. Teachers typically focus on a particular topic (e.g., volume of three-dimensional figures), use a particular resource (e.g., Periodic Table of Elements), and choose specific instructional methods (e.g., problem-based learning) to cause learning that meets a given standard. However, each of these decisions is actually a step in a learning process that should end in a performance by the student to demonstrate learning. Student activity without an end performance in mind is often busy work. Instruction, no matter how engaging or intellectual, is only beneficial if it ends with students demonstrating their knowledge and skills resulting from the learning experience. A performance approach to curriculum planning should begin with the specific student performance.

This backwards approach to curricular design also departs from another unfortunate but common practice: thinking about assessment as something to plan at the end, after teaching is completed. Rather than creating assessments near the conclusion of a unit of study (or relying on the tests provided by textbook publishers, which may not assess state standards completely or appropriately), backwards design calls for thinking about the work students will produce and how it might be assessed as you begin to plan a unit or course. Once you focus on a clear student performance, it is easier to select appropriate instructional strategies that will help students achieve that performance.

There are four major steps in planning rigorous and relevant instruction:

1. Define the focus of learning.
2. Create the student performance.
3. Design the assessment.
4. Develop the learning experiences.

The four steps are presented in the order in which ideal planning should occur. You select appropriate strategies in Step 4, after defining the focus, student performance, and assessment.

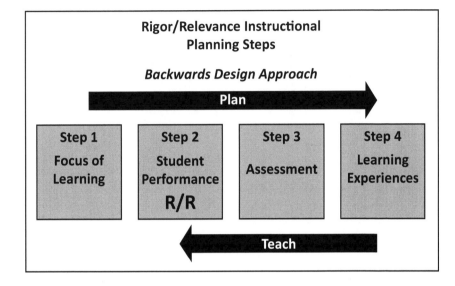

Selecting Strategies

The appropriateness of using any of the instructional strategies described in this handbook in individual situations depends upon matching the characteristics of the strategy, the learners, and what needs to be learned. All of these factors should be considered when selecting the best strategy for the learning situation. The more familiar you are with the strategies, the more likely you are to select the best strategy.

Although each strategy is described separately, the strategies are rarely used independently. When creating instructional units, you will typically select several strategies. For example, a lecture may precede a demonstration and ultimately lead to a problem-based exercise. Keeping in mind the strengths of each strategy will help you to create effective instructional experiences for your students.

Writing Strategies and the Rigor/Relevance Framework

The first criterion to consider in selecting writing strategies is the level of student performance. When students are expected to demonstrate high levels of complex use of knowledge, then the instructional strategy used must give students experience with complex use of knowledge. In contrast, if students are only expected to recall knowledge, then the selected strategy can be simple, straightforward instruction. High levels of student performance often require application of knowledge.

Again, the instruction needs to match this level of expectation and give students learning experiences in which they apply knowledge.

The best way to develop a systematic approach to matching instructional strategy to the expected level of student performance is through the knowledge taxonomy and application model in the Rigor/Relevance Framework. The instructional strategies can be related to a particular quadrant of the Rigor/Relevance Framework. Likewise, the expected levels of student performance can be related to the Rigor/Relevance Framework. Select instructional strategies that work best for the quadrant in which your student objectives are located. When used at the right time, these strategies can help students to achieve expected standards.

 # Analogies

For the Teacher

Defining the Strategy

"She drank in the last five pages like a fish gulping in the lake water after rescuing itself from the bottom of a fishing boat." This analogy emphasizes the voraciousness with which the character read the last five pages of her book. The writer could have simply written that the character read the last five pages of her book quickly and excitedly, but that would not have had the same effect or meaning. The analogy implies that she was so engrossed in those pages that nothing else in the world mattered. The outside world stopped. The analogy helps the reader to understand the character exactly how the writer intends.

An analogy compares two things that are different, in order to highlight how they are the same. Analogies are used to clarify. By comparing something unfamiliar to something familiar, a writer can help a reader to better understand the unfamiliar. Analogies are also used to enhance writing. An analogy can aid the writer in describing something in ways that are not possible with only adjectives. In analogy writing, students learn how to convey complex ideas and information more clearly, think creatively, and develop their writing in ways that are appropriate to their task and purpose.

Analogy writing also increases the level of rigorous and relevant thinking. It requires students to apply prior knowledge and think in complex ways about how things are related. Analogy writing fits clearly within Quadrant D on the Rigor/Relevance Framework as it includes the higher ends of both the Knowledge Taxonomy and the Application Model. To understand an analogy, students will use analysis, synthesis, and evaluation. In addition, they will apply their knowledge to real-world situations, such as understanding human anatomy or government functions. As they write analogies, they may find themselves applying knowledge to real-world unpredictable situations as well.

Applying the Strategy

Analogy writing is used across the board in the three main areas of writing according to the Common Core State Standards: narrative writing, informative/explanatory writing, and argument writing. In each type of writing, the purpose of the analogy remains the same—to make something clearer to the reader. This writing strategy specifically relates to standards 1 and 9 of the Common Core College and Career Anchor Standards for Writing. Standard 1 focuses on the writing of arguments to support claims and the analysis of substantive topics or texts, using valid reasoning and relevant sufficient evidence. When making an argument, an analogy can prove very useful. A reader may have a difficult time seeing something from the writer's point of view and an analogy that simplifies can sway the reader in the writer's direction.

Anchor standard 9 covers the drawing of evidence from literary or informational texts to support analysis, reflection, and research. This is a clearly useful place for the use of analogies. An analogy can help clarify a writer's reflection on, or analysis of, a literary text. Analogies can also help simplify concepts in an informational text.

Analogy writing is an effective strategy in most content areas and in middle and secondary programs. It can be particularly useful in science. Research has shown that using analogies to teach and explain difficult science concepts improves comprehension and retention.

Middle School

- Science
    - explaining ecosystems by comparing them to cities or towns
    - comparing blood vessels to highways

- Social Studies
  - describing government structures by comparing them to sharing a house and responsibilities within a family
- Math
  - describing balancing an equation like balancing a scale
  - relating operations with numbers to operations with variables
- ELA
  - clarifying relationships among ideas and concepts
  - using precise language and vocabulary

Secondary School

- Science
  - understanding the cell and how it functions
  - comprehending energy in the earth system
- Social Studies
  - understanding the relationship of the United States to other nations and world affairs
  - understanding roles of citizens in a democracy
- Math
  - understanding structure in expressions
  - comprehending arithmetic operations in relation to polynomials
- ELA
  - organizing complex ideas, concepts, and information to make important connections and distinctions
  - using precise language and vocabulary to convey a vivid picture of experiences, events, settings, or characters

Common Core State Standards

College and Career Readiness Anchor Standards for Writing

Text Types and Purposes

2. Write informative/explanatory texts to examine and convey complex ideas and information clearly and accurately through the effective selection, organization, and analysis of content.

3. Write narratives to develop real or imagined experiences or events using effective technique, well-chosen details, and well-structured event sequences.

Production and Distribution of Writing

4. Produce clear and coherent writing in which the development, organization, and style are appropriate to task, purpose, and audience.

5. Develop and strengthen writing as needed by planning, revising, editing, rewriting, or trying a new approach.

Research to Build and Present Knowledge

9. Draw evidence from literary or informational texts to support analysis, reflection, and research.

Teaching the Strategy

Introduce the strategy by explaining the main uses of analogies:

- **To clarify.** Analogies are used to clarify more complex ideas by comparing them to familiar ideas. The reader can then make connections between what they know and the unfamiliar concept to help them make sense of the unfamiliar concept.

- **To enhance communication and writing.** The analogy given on the first page comparing the reader to a fish that had just returned to water helps the audience know exactly what the writer means. The analogy, moreover, brightens and enlivens the writing, making it more interesting for the reader. In this case, the writer takes a familiar concept, reading a book, and connects it to a very different concept to convey meaning.

Writing an analogy requires creative thinking. Writers must stretch the imagination to create analogies. Different tools can be helpful to the student looking for ways to create analogies.

- **Concept Map.** A concept map allows students to show how ideas are related. A main idea or topic is often listed in the middle circle, and supporting details that support that topic are listed in the other circles. A concept map is useful for identifying characteristics of an unfamiliar concept. For example, if a writer wanted to explain a complex concept like photosynthesis, they could first use a concept map to list the characteristics or steps in photosynthesis. This will help them identify which parts of photosynthesis are similar to more familiar concepts.

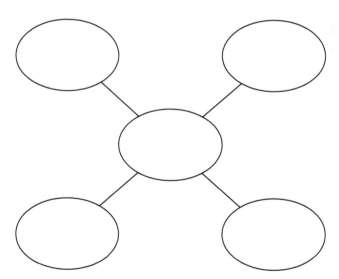

- **Analogy Graphic Organizer.** Sometimes a writer will have two things they would like to compare in an analogy, but may need help clarifying their thinking. In this case, a graphic organizer such as the one below can be helpful. The writer can use the organizer to help them think about how the two things are similar and different and then narrow the characteristics they want to highlight in the analogy.

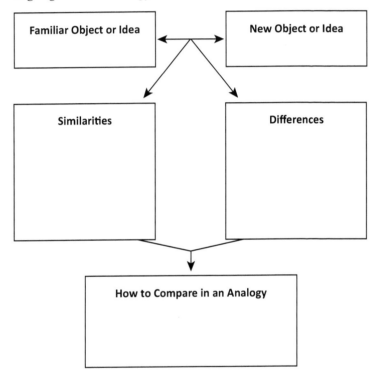

- **Sentence Starters.** When using an analogy to enliven writing, a writer most often begins with a more familiar concept. To practice writing these kinds of analogies, use sentence starters to help students think about how aspects of familiar topics can be described in analogies.

- I feel like…
- My dog is like…
- School is like…
- A thunderstorm is like…

When students are first working on writing analogies, it may also be helpful for them to add the word "because" to a sentence starter to help them identify a similarity. For example, "School is like _____ because _____."

When writing an analogy, it is important to know your audience and understand the limits of an analogy. For example, the familiar concept must be familiar to the audience. If a writer uses a concept that is too complex, the reader will not understand the analogy. In addition, writers need to remember that even though they are comparing two different things in an analogy, there must be enough similarity for the analogy to work. To claim that a dog waiting at the door for its owner is like an eagle swooping down to capture its prey does not work. The dog is anticipating a reunion, while the eagle is anticipating lunch.

Directed Writing Activity

1. This activity will challenge students to write analogies. It will gradually move them from using sentence starters to writing complete analogies.

2. Write the following sentence starter on the board:

   A camera is like a/an _____ because _____.

3. Have students work with a partner or in small groups to brainstorm ideas for an object or idea with which to complete the first blank of the sentence starter. Choose your own object or idea to complete the blank. Then have students choose how to complete each analogy on their own by completing the second blank.

4. Now that each student has two things they are comparing, have them complete an analogy graphic organizer to define the similarities and differences between the two things. First, develop a class graphic organizer using the two ideas or objects in the sen-

tence starter on the board. The camera will be the "new" object. Then have students complete the graphic organizer on their own.

5. Look at the class graphic organizer again and use the similarities and differences to write an analogy as a class. Point out that an analogy can be longer than one sentence.

6. Have students share their analogies. Have the other students identify the thread of similarity in each analogy.

7. Assign the independent writing activity.

References

Glynn, S. M.. "Explaining Science Concepts: A Teaching-with-Analogies Model," in S. M. Glynn, R. H. Yeany, and B. K. Britton (Eds.), *The Psychology of Learning Science* (pp. 219–240). Hillsdale, NJ: Erlbaum, 1991.

James, Mark C., Scharmann, Lawrence C."Using Analogies to Improve the Teaching Performance of Preservice Teachers." *Journal of Research in Science Teaching*, Vol. 44, Issue 4, pp. 565–585), 2007.

For the Student

Independent Writing Activity

Follow these directions to practice writing analogies. Use specific vocabulary and well-chosen details in your analogies. Think carefully about how to convey complex ideas clearly and accurately. Develop your writing appropriately by planning, revising, and editing.

1. Choose one of the following topics, or another similarly complex topic, and write an analogy to explain its meaning.

    *   a science topic such as evaporation of water in the water cycle or migration of animals

    *   writing an introductory paragraph for an essay, or another part of the writing process

    *   the rules of a sport

    *   using a computer program

    *   the rules of a specific game

2. Use a concept map to identify the characteristics or main points of the topic. Use these ideas to help you decide what to compare the topic to in an analogy.

3. Complete an analogy graphic organizer for the two things you will compare in your analogy. Write a first draft of an analogy.

    Sample answer: Winter vacationers are like birds flying south—they're both in search of warmer weather.

4. Revise your analogy. Can you use more precise vocabulary? Is the connection clear? Does the simpler topic help explain the more complex topic?

    Sample answer: Snowbirds, people that move south for the winter, are like actual birds — both migrate to warmer weather.

Concept Map

Add circles if necessary.

Concept Map

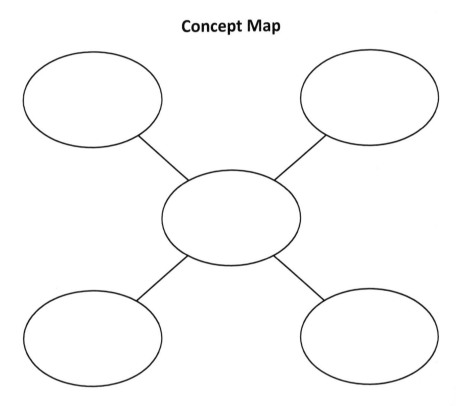

Analogy Organizer

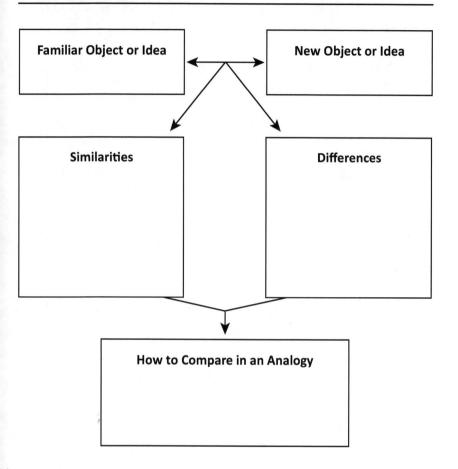

Familiar Object or Idea		New Object or Idea

Similarities	Differences

How to Compare in an Analogy

Sample Analogy Organizer

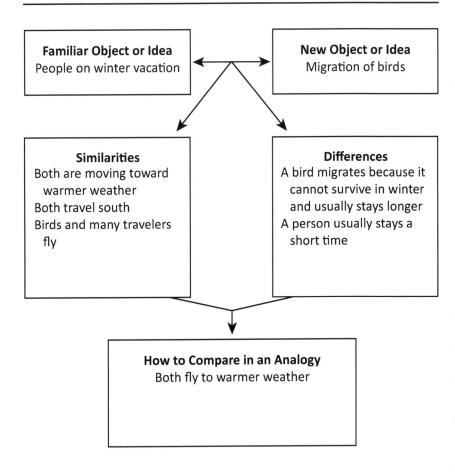

Familiar Object or Idea
People on winter vacation

New Object or Idea
Migration of birds

Similarities
Both are moving toward warmer weather
Both travel south
Birds and many travelers fly

Differences
A bird migrates because it cannot survive in winter and usually stays longer
A person usually stays a short time

How to Compare in an Analogy
Both fly to warmer weather

Analytic Academic Writing

For the Teacher

Defining the Strategy

The primary writing task students face is the formal analytic academic essay or theme/term paper. This differs from the traditional high school essay, which lacks the sophistication and flexibility of a college paper. The writer is required to break down a subject or topic to its essential parts and draw fresh conclusions based on research while demonstrating critical thinking. This may seem a daunting task, but at its core, academic writing is simply a thorough analysis of what the writer has learned. This demands clear thinking and writing, an intriguing and arguable thesis, as well as coherent, focused paragraphs that build a structure of ideas within the conventions of the academic paper. The topic of this work must be relevant, appropriate, and focused on teaching the reader something new and useful about a topic. This task can take the form of arguing with the reader, informing the reader, or telling the reader a story.

Analytical academic essays require extensive research to support a thesis or claim with valid reasoning and relevant and sufficient evidence from multiple authoritative print and digital sources. They also must maintain a formal style with a concluding statement that supports the argument presented. Some employ a narrative containing well-organized event sequences that have a smooth progression and one or multiple points of view. All employ clear and coherent writing in which the development, organization, and style are appropriate to the task and purpose.

Academic writing requires students to move through a variety of inter-related types of thinking, which can be fruitfully understood in terms of the Rigor/Relevance Framework. The construction of a workable thesis and identification of an audience, for instance, falls within Quadrant B. As students conduct a thorough analysis of their topic by writing an essay, they are devising unique solutions for deeper understanding of unpredictable problems and demonstrating their assimilation of acquired knowledge in Quadrant C. In applying knowledge and skills from research, they provide an analytical clarification of something previously unknown and link the formerly confusing connections among the ideas they presenting. Their final drafts are Quadrant D extensions that further develop their skills and knowledge.

Common Core State Standards

College and Career Readiness Anchor Standards for Writing

Text Types and Purposes

1. Write arguments to support your claims in an analysis of substantive topics or texts, using valid reasoning and relevant and sufficient evidence.

2. Write informative/explanatory texts to examine and convey complex ideas and information clearly and accurately through the effective selection, organization, and analysis of content.

3. Write narratives to develop real or imagined experiences or events using effective technique, well-chosen details, and well-structured event sequences.

Production and Distribution of Writing

4. Produce clear and coherent writing in which the development, organization, and style are appropriate to task, purpose, and audience.

5. Develop and strengthen writing as needed by planning, revising, editing, rewriting, or trying a new approach.

Research to Build and Present Knowledge

6. Conduct short as well as more sustained research projects based on focused questions, demonstrating your understanding of the subject under investigation.

7. Gather relevant information from multiple print and digital sources, assess the credibility and accuracy of each source, and integrate the information while avoiding plagiarism.

8. Draw evidence from literary or informational texts to support analysis, reflection, and research.

Applying the Strategy

Analytic academic writing is an effective strategy across most content areas in middle and secondary programs.

Middle School

- Science
  - lab reports
  - analysis of scientific accomplishments
  - term papers on scientific explanations of natural phenomena
- Social Studies
  - biographies of historical figures
  - narrative accounts of events in history
  - clarifications of the separation of powers
- Math
  - explanations of mathematic concepts
  - narrating steps in a geometric proof
- ELA
  - exploring personal reactions to fiction, short stories, memoirs, diaries, eyewitness accounts
  - formal term papers about literary trends

Secondary School

- Science
  - comparisons of the functions of different bodily systems
  - reports on cell functions and biochemistry
  - descriptions of wave and light behavior
- Social Studies
  - historical accounts constructed from primary sources
  - surveys of different historians' views
  - citations of competing anthropological explanations of human behavior
- Math
  - explanations of different properties
  - interpretations of statistics and polling percentages
- ELA
  - analysis of poetic styles and rhyme schemes
  - deconstruction of literary styles
  - narrative accounts of an artist's lifework
  - character analysis
- Exposition used in the workplace
  - business reports
  - memoranda
  - oral academic presentations
  - business talks and speeches

Teaching the Strategy

Introduce the strategy by explaining that there are three types of analytical academic writing: argument, informative/explanatory, and narrative.

- **Argument.** The writer stakes a claim or position on an issue or topic and then proceeds to provide reasons and evidence to support that claim. With all analytical writing, students will express a belief about a subject, such as their analysis of a book or their interpretation of historical events and then back up their argument with facts and details that prove their point. Counterarguments should be introduced and refuted in the process of drawing conclusions or calling the reader to action.

- **Informative/Explanatory.** This type of writing can take many forms and is often referred to as expository writing. It explains information to a reader. As analytic writing, it exposes the component parts of an idea or an issue by breaking the idea down and evaluating it. Comparison-and-contrast, problem-solution, cause-and-effect, sequence, and description are some of the basic formats employed in this type of writing. Examples include proposals for a business, professional opinions, discussions of current trends, or arguments about historical records.

- **Narrative.** Storytelling is perhaps the oldest form of writing. It is both personal to the author as well as involving for the reader. The writer relates a sequence of events, anecdotes, and experiences in a highly creative and emotionally satisfying manner. Narrative form can take the traditional story form of introduction, plot, characters, setting, climax, and conclusion or take the form of an essay with a theme or thesis that is illustrated by parts of the narration. The famous first day of school essay, "What I Did on My Summer Vacation" must still have a purpose, a recognizable point of view, strong organization, concise word usage, and description. Narrative format is also analytical in a travelogue that illustrates the author's understanding of what it means to be an atypical tourist or in a series of vignettes that probes how children today are forced to grow up too quickly.

In an argumentative research paper, the writer takes a stance on a debatable subject and stakes a claim, "Prescribing too many antibiotics is a serious health hazard." An analytical research paper functions as informative or explanatory writing and begins with a student asking a question that generates research. The writer does not take a stance, only poses an inquiry, such as, "How is the reader supposed to interpret *The Canterbury Tales*? In a narrative academic writing, the writer tells a story to illustrate a point, "My journey through the wilds of high school in the inner city."

Checklist for Beginning Analytical Academic Writing

All types of analytical writing can be characterized as sharing common traits. Review these questions and attributes before selecting a topic:

- What does this mean? How is it important? Why does it work? What do others think?
- To what audience am I speaking? How can I use my research to interest them? Will they believe me?
- Can I define my topic, issue, or problem? Is my purpose clear? Am I probing deeply enough into relationships?
- Have I interpreted a set of events? Investigated a problem? Described how something developed? Pointed out something that has been overlooked or misunderstood? Explained an interaction, trend, or underlying principle?

Requirements of the Research Paper

1. Research, outline, draft, revise, edit, proofread.
2. Summarize, evaluate, analyze, synthesize.
3. Form an intellectual question and provide a complex, thoughtful answer.
4. Take a stand on a topic, adopt a rhetorical stance, maintain tone and style.
5. Provide an argument and exposition: an introduction, a thesis sentence, supporting paragraphs with each containing a topic

sentence and evidence, other sides of the argument, and a conclusion.

6. Make a sketch or graphic that presents a diagram of connections between ideas and then develop this as an outline.

7. Provide in narrative format: introduction, plot, characters, setting, climax, and conclusion.

8. Support claims for arguments with valid reasoning and relevant and sufficient evidence.

9. Assess the credibility and accuracy of research from multiple print and digital sources.

10. Support arguments, analysis, or storytelling with evidence from either literary or informational texts without plagiarizing.

Three Format Matrices

Use any of the three matrices that follow as an organizer for each of the three types of analytical writing.

Elements of Argument

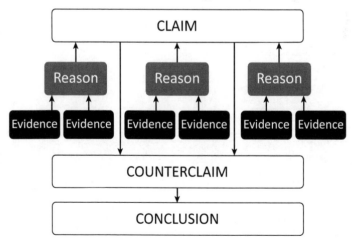

Expository Essay Graphic Organizer

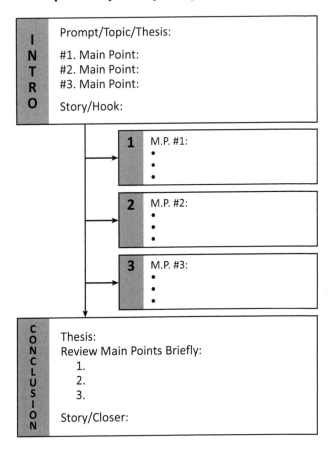

Narrative Organizer

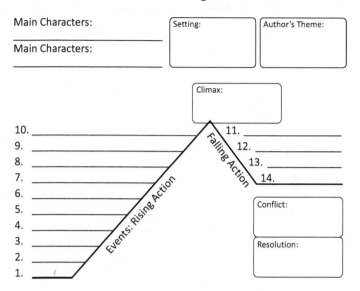

Main Characters: _____

Main Characters: _____

Setting:

Author's Theme:

Climax:

10. _____
9. _____
8. _____
7. _____
6. _____
5. _____
4. _____
3. _____
2. _____
1. _____

Events: Rising Action

Falling Action

11. _____
12. _____
13. _____
14. _____

Conflict:

Resolution:

Directed Writing Activity

1. This activity will require students to produce clear and coherent writing in which development, organization, and style are suited to task and purpose. Display the graphic organizers. Start with the Expository Essay organizer, which uses the same basic format as a narrative or argumentative essay. Students can select one of the other organizers if they wish, but should follow along as the class completes the sample organizer.

2. Emphasize to the class that if they were writing a complete expository essay, they would have to do extensive research to provide the evidence and detail that the essay would demand. For demonstration purposes, use the novel *The Old Man and The Sea*, which most students have read and know well. Note that you are only demonstrating elements of the expository essay form that students might use.

3. Ask students to look over the expository graphic organizer. The introduction at the very top left corner is paired with the conclu-

sion at the bottom. Remind students that both the introduction and conclusion state the thesis or topic, which can also be used as a prompt to begin discussions. Both also state the main points, which are fully elaborated in the paragraphs that form the body of the essay. Encourage students to be creative with each of these parts. They should not just list these ideas, but present them in an engaging and unique manner to entertain their readers. Remind students that they can develop their organizer with considerable variation from this model.

4. Beginning with the topic, remind students that in this essay they will be analyzing or breaking down an idea and evaluating it. They should also go through the checklist above to define their work, identify a potential audience, and be prepared to explain their ideas.

5. Discuss possible topics, stressing that students should select an idea they could explain, like why the novel has remained so popular when it is such a simple story about a fisherman and a trophy fish. Invite discussion but add the thesis or topic shown in the class organizer below.

6. Discuss an introduction that will both catch the reader's attention and encapsulate the essence of the story. It should also preview what you are explaining.

7. Review the suggested entries for the thesis, main ideas, and the topic sentences. Point out how they fulfill the definition of each element and then provide an analytic breakdown of the thesis by demonstrating each point with facts and details from the novel.

8. Note how the Common Core State Standards for Writing are met by introducing the topic clearly; previewing; organizing ideas into broader categories; developing the topic with facts, details, quotations, and examples; clarifying relationships among concepts; using precise language; maintaining a formal style; and providing a conclusion that supports the explanation.

9. After learners complete their graphic organizers, review and discuss the assignment. Ask students how they would organize their essays differently if they had used the template for Argument or Narrative. Then assign the independent writing activity.

Sample Expository Essay Graphic Organizer

INTRO

Introduction: The worst kind of luck befalls a fisherman who can't catch a fish for weeks and then hooks a giant marlin.

Thesis: Why has *The Old Man and The Sea* remained so popular and enduring?

Main Idea #1: The fisherman, Santiago, is cursed with bad luck but overcomes this with success.

Main Idea #2: After hooking a giant marlin, he endures great physical pain but catching this fish will change his luck, fulfill a dream, and give his life meaning in his old age.

Main Idea #3: Although sharks destroy his fish, Santiago has won the greater battle of courage and determination and he has earned respect.

1

Paragraph #1: Topic Sentence: Santiago's apprentice, Manolin, is no longer allowed to fish with him because he is cursed, yet Santiago has refused to give up his career and greets each day with the quote, "Every day is a new day," and indeed that day changes everything.

Detail: Eighty-four straight days without catching a fish.

Evidence: The quote is proof that despite his luck he hasn't lost confidence and determination.

2

Paragraph #2: Topic Sentence: Santiago knows that if he can endure, he will have saved himself and avoided the ridicule he will face if the fish defeats him.

Detail: The marlin drags him for two days and the rope cuts his hands.

Evidence: It would be easy to give up on the fish and on his life but he says, "I'll try it again."

3

Paragraph #3: Catching the fish becomes less important than not giving up and even though he brings in only a carcass, his endurance proves he is not cursed and that his life has been worthwhile.

Detail: His battle lasts three days and nights but within hours the sharks attack.

Evidence: As Santiago talks to Manolin after he limps home, he plans for future adventures.

CONCLUSION

Conclusion: Repeat Thesis: The novel has been popular because it tells more than the story of a man fighting a fish. It demonstrates that life demands impossible struggle and that even in apparent defeat, humans win by surviving and not giving up so they can enjoy another day.

Review Main Ideas: Santiago's luck finally changes but only at a great physical toll as he understands that his dream of first catching, then bringing the marlin home to cheers is gone, but it is replaced by the respect he earns by not giving up, which gives him justification for his entire life.

Reference

Jones, R. *Rigor and Relevance Handbook*. Rexford, NY: International Center for Leadership in Education, 2010.

For the Student

Independent Writing Activity

Follow these directions to write an argument, information/explanation, or narrative essay. Develop your writing appropriately by planning, revising, and editing.

1. Decide on a topic or select one of the suggestions here. Match the topic to the graphic organizer you use. If research materials are available, preview the research and formulate a topic. Textbooks, magazines, or short stories could be used. The following are suggested topics:

   - an argument about controversial school policy

   - an explanation of your personal style in clothing and hairdo

   - a story from your childhood that taught you something

   - an argument about why you liked or disliked a movie or book

   - a series of stories that demonstrate one of life's lessons

2. If you are unable to research your topic, choose a thesis you know well enough to provide details and evidence. Remember to be analytical and break down the topic so as to thoroughly investigate it. Match your analysis to your audience. Interpret your ideas for your reader.

3. Complete a graphic organizer showing your organization of ideas.

4. Write an essay of five short paragraphs. Use the same format and methodology as a longer analytic academic essay.

Comparison-Contrast Matrix

	Item 1	Item 2
Characteristic 1		
Characteristic 2		
Characteristic 3		
Characteristic 4		
Characteristic 5		
Characteristic 6		
Characteristic 7		
Characteristic 8		

Venn Diagram

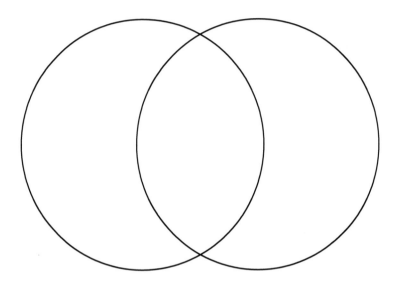

▙ Analytical Writing Models

For the Teacher

Defining the Strategy

The Common Core State Standards place an emphasis on producing complex analytical writing that combines writing types. This emphasis is aligned with the fact that analytical writing is the writing most often required in college or professions.

Analytical writing:

- asks and answers thought-provoking questions such as, "What does it mean?" "How does it work?" "Why is it this way?"
- analyzes
- synthesizes and evaluates information
- considers the audience
- offers a different perspective from the reader's experience
- develops critical thinking, problem solving, and deep understanding
- relies on argument, informative, and narrative writing

To learn to write analytically, students will first dissect analytical writing models. The main point in deconstructing texts is for students to develop clear expectations for their own writing. Deconstructing and analyzing models will answer questions such as, "How do I develop and organize an argument?" "How can I convey a complex idea to my readers?" "How do I analyze information to form my own opinion?" "How do I combine writing types?"

The level of rigorous and relevant thinking involved in analytical thinking is high. It requires students to think in complex ways and apply their knowledge to new situations. This fact lands it squarely within Quadrant D on the Rigor/Relevance Framework. Students are not only looking at writing that analyzes — they are themselves analyzing and evaluating the writing. Doing so will require them to read critically and make decisions using their knowledge of analytical writing.

Applying the Strategy

This strategy specifically relates to standards 1, 8, and 9 of the Common Core College and Career Anchor Standards for Writing. Anchor standard 1 asks that students "Write arguments to support claims in an analysis of substantive topics or texts, using valid reasoning and relevant sufficient evidence." When students analyze analytical writing models, they identify reasoning and evidence used to support an argument.

Anchor standard 8 asks students to "Gather relevant information from multiple print and digital sources, assess the credibility and accuracy of each source, and integrate the information while avoiding plagiarism." Although students are not gathering information when analyzing analytical writing models, they are assessing the credibility and accuracy of the sources.

Anchor standard 9 requires students to "Draw evidence from literary or informational texts to support analysis, reflection, and research." When deconstructing an analytical writing model, students learn to identify evidence. This, in turn, helps them understand how to use evidence in analytical writing to support their argument.

Deconstructing an analytical writing model is a useful strategy to use before beginning an analytical writing task. It can serve both as a learning tool to zero in on the characteristics of analytical writing or as a refresher or reminder.

Middle School

- Science
  - finding evidence
  - exploring models and providing explanations
- Social Studies
  - analyzing historical documents for bias
- Math
  - analyzing statistics
  - developing probability experiments
- ELA
  - introducing claims and supporting them with logical reasoning
  - clarifying the relationships among claims, reasons, and evidence

Secondary School

- Science
  - conducting scientific inquiries
  - understanding the abilities of science and technology
- Social Studies
  - dissecting historical documents such as the Magna Carta, the Declaration of Independence, and so on
- Math
  - analyzing proofs
  - deconstructing the reasoning given for solving equations
- ELA
  - writing arguments to support claims
  - identifying relationships among claims and reasons, reasons and evidence, claims and counterclaims

Common Core State Standards

College and Career Readiness Anchor Standards for Writing

Text Types and Purposes

1. Write arguments to support claims in an analysis of substantive topics or texts, using valid reasoning and relevant and sufficient evidence.

2. Write informative/explanatory texts to examine and convey complex ideas and information clearly and accurately through the effective selection, organization, and analysis of content.

3. Write narratives to develop real or imagined experiences or events using effective techniques, well-chosen details, and well-structured event sequences.

Production and Distribution of Writing

4. Produce clear and coherent writing in which the development, organization, and style are appropriate to task, purpose, and audience.

5. Develop and strengthen writing as needed by planning, revising, editing, rewriting, or trying a new approach.

6. Use technology, including the Internet, to produce and publish writing and to interact and collaborate with others.

Research to Build and Present Knowledge

7. Conduct short as well as more sustained research projects based on focused questions, and thereby demonstrate an understanding of the subject under investigation.

8. Gather relevant information from multiple print and digital sources, assess the credibility and accuracy of each source, and integrate the information while avoiding plagiarism.

9. Draw evidence from literary or informational texts to support analysis, reflection, and research.

Range of Writing

10. Write routinely over extended time frames (with time for research, reflection, and revision) and shorter time frames (a single sitting or a day or two) for a range of tasks, purposes, and audiences.

Teaching the Strategy

Introduce the strategy by reiterating the three main types of analytical writing. It is important before students analyze a writing model that they understand the writing type they are using. Point out that some pieces of writing contain more than one type of writing within the same piece.

- **Argument.** In an argument, the writer argues a claim that they support with one or more convincing reasons.

- **Informative/explanatory.** This is nonfiction writing that gives information about a topic including who, what, where, when, why, and how.

- **Narrative.** A narrative is a story about a real or fictional experience.

Follow these steps when helping students analyze a model text:

1. **Introduce the model of analytical writing.** Describe the type of writing — argument, informative/explanatory, or narrative — and explain how it is organized. Discuss specific aspects of the writing type. The writing type will help students understand what writing elements to look for in the text.

2. **Read the writing model.** You can read the model aloud, or use an Oral Cloze or Partner Cloze routine, or some combination thereof. Students should read the model more than once to become familiar with it.

3. **Teach the writing elements.** Guide students to find them in the model.

When students analyze a writing model, set clear instructions for annotating the model. For example:

- **Number** or label the paragraphs.
- **Underline** the writer's claim or thesis statement.
- **Place arrows** next to the reasons for the claim.
- **Place stars** next to the evidence that supports the reasons for the claim.
- **Put a box** around the counterclaim or counterclaims.
- **Place checkmarks** next to the quotations and citations.
- **Circle** the recommendation or call to action.
- **Circle** transition words and precise adjectives or adverbs.

Directed Writing Activity

1. This activity will require students to analyze an analytical writing model as a class. While working with students, take the opportunity to deconstruct the text thoroughly. The more they understand the writing, the better they will be able to write analytically on their own.

2. Give each student a copy of the text "Harmless Media Images" by Anthony Simpson. Inform students that this is an argument paper about teens and media images. Use the Oral Cloze routine to read the text aloud. Then have students read it a second time on their own.

3. As a group, annotate the text following the instructions below. As you proceed through each writing element, encourage discussion about what a claim is, what reasons and evidence are, why citations are important, and so on.
   - **Number or label** the paragraphs.
   - **Underline** the writer's claim or thesis statement.
   - **Place arrows** next to the reasons for the claim.
   - **Place stars** next to the evidence that supports the reasons for the claim.

- **Put a box** around the counterclaim or counterclaims.
- **Place checkmarks** next to the quotations and citations.
- **Circle** the recommendation or call to action.
- **Circle** transition words and precise adjectives or adverbs.

4. Discuss with students the value of analyzing a text. Ask them to describe how this process will help them improve their writing. What was new to them? What do they think they will incorporate into their own writing?

5. Assign the independent writing activity.

Sample Annotated Text

Harmless Media Images
by Anthony Simpson

① After examining the issues surrounding the media and self-image, I agree wholeheartedly that the media are not responsible for teens' body images. Therefore media images should not be regulated and be restricted for teenagers.

② One reason I maintain this position is that the media often show healthy images. In the article "The Ugly Effects of Beauty," Marcus Cano presents compelling data regarding the positive effect of media images. For example, the editor of *Men's Health* explains that his magazine shows what fit men look like (Cano 57). ✓ ★

③ Critics of these images tend to point out that they make boys take extreme measures (Cano 56). However, to subscribe to the notion that media images damage boys' health is unfounded. Studies actually demonstrate that only 2 percent of boys use steroids (Allegre 28). ✓ ★

④ I am also opposed to regulating media images due to teens' knowledge that the images are not real. Pedro Gutierrez emphasizes in his essay, "The Image Artist," that retouching creates ideal images to sell products (Gutierrez 60). One particularly convincing statistic is that female models typically "weigh 23 percent less than the average woman" (Cano 55). ✓ ★

⑤ Whether media images harm teens will no doubt remain a controversial issue. After reviewing relevant data and reflecting on my own experiences as an adolescent, I still contend that the media cannot be held accountable for teens' self-images.

For the Student

Independent Writing Activity

Follow these directions to deconstruct an analytical writing model.

1. Read the excerpt "Global Warming" by Sir John Houghton. The first time, simply read the text. The second time, pay greater attention to the writing elements and also to what type of text it is or what types of text it combines.

2. What type of writing is this? Explain.

   Sample answer: It is informative text as well as an argument.

   It presents the argument that global warming is largely the

   result of human activities but also provides data and

   information about the actual changes in the temperature of

   the earth the last 20,000 years.

3. Use the following instructions to annotate the text as you analyze it.

   - **Number or label** the paragraphs.
   - **Underline** the writer's claim or thesis statement.
   - **Place arrows** next to the reasons for the claim.
   - **Place stars** next to the evidence that supports the reasons for the claim.
   - **Put a box** around the counterclaim or counterclaims.
   - **Place checkmarks** next to the quotations and citations.
   - **Circle** the recommendation or call to action.
   - **Circle** transition words and precise adjectives or adverbs.

4. Do you think the author makes a valid claim? Why or why not?

   Sample answer: I do think the author makes a valid claim.

   There is enough evidence to suggest that humans are causing

   global warming.

5. Do you think there is sufficient evidence to support his claim? Explain.

   Yes, the fossil fuel burning that came about with the Industrial

   Revolution combined with the fact that the greenhouse effect

   has changed most dramatically since the 1800s supports his

   claim.

6. This is an excerpt, without a conclusion. What recommendations do you think the author would most likely make?

   Sample answer: I think he would most likely recommend

   changes to how we use fossil fuels and the amount of

   greenhouse gases that humans produce.

7. Share your annotations with a partner. Discuss each writing element and its strengths. Could it be improved? How would you change it?

Sample Annotations

Harmless Media Images
by Anthony Simpson

① After examining the issues surrounding the media and self-image, I agree wholeheartedly that the media are not responsible for teens' body images. Therefore media images should not be regulated and be restricted for teenagers.

② One reason I maintain this position is that the media often show healthy images. In the article "The Ugly Effects of Beauty," Marcus Cano presents compelling data regarding the positive effect of media images. For example, the editor of *Men's Health* explains that his magazine shows what fit men look like (Cano 57). ✓ ★

③ Critics of these images tend to point out that they make boys take extreme measures (Cano 56). However, to subscribe to the notion that media images damage boys' health is unfounded. Studies actually demonstrate that only 2 percent of boys use steroids (Allegre 28). ✓ ★

④ I am also opposed to regulating media images due to teens' knowledge that the images are not real. Pedro Gutierrez emphasizes in his essay, "The Image Artist," that retouching creates ideal images to sell products (Gutierrez 60). One particularly convincing statistic is that female models typically "weigh 23 percent less than the average woman" (Cano 55). ✓ ★

⑤ Whether media images harm teens will no doubt remain a controversial issue. After reviewing relevant data and reflecting on my own experiences as an adolescent, I still contend that the media cannot be held accountable for teens' self-images.

Global Warming
by Sir John Houghton

① The term "global warming" is used by the general public to refer to the phenomenon of global change arising from human activities that result in an increase in greenhouse gases, notably carbon dioxide, in the atmosphere. One manifestation of this climate change is the observed rise in global mean temperature at Earth's surface. This climate change involves much more than just increases in global temperatures, however. Changes in precipitation, drought, and water resources, for instance, are also involved. Such factors can have a (profound) impact on the environment and human endeavors.

② The increase in temperatures cannot be entirely explained by natural cycles. It is (largely) the result of human activities. Chief among these activities is the burning of fossil fuels, which include coal, oil, and gasoline. When these fuels are burned, they release gases that act like the glass in a greenhouse. They trap heat in Earth's atmosphere. These gases — which include water vapor, carbon dioxide, and methane — are called greenhouse gases.

③ These gases enhance the natural "greenhouse effect." This effect was recognized about 200 years ago and keeps Earth's surface about 36 Fahrenheit degrees (20 Celsius degrees) warmer than it would otherwise be.

④ The greenhouse effect (scarcely) changed for thousands of years. This was because the levels of greenhouse gases remained stable. However, one of these gases, carbon dioxide, started a (dramatic) increase in the 1800s. The increase was due to the burning of large amounts of fossil fuels during the Industrial Revolution. Since then, the burning of fossil fuels has increased. More greenhouse gases have entered the atmosphere, and temperatures have continued to rise. There is some debate as to how much of climate change is caused by humans. Some people who doubt that human activities cause global warming say that climate changes could be due to changes in the Sun's output. But in 2007 a study revealed that the Sun's output has been decreasing since 1985, even though global temperatures have been rising ever faster.

Gathering Evidence

⑤ It is common for temperature and climate trends to change for natural reasons — that is, for reasons that have nothing to do with human activities. Natural reasons are not enough to explain global warming, however. Natural climate cycles tend to unfold slowly but the changes seen with global warming are relatively sudden.

⑥ Over the past 1,000 years, temperature changes have fit within a range defined by two extreme periods: a warm period, which took place about 1200 to 1400, and a "little ice age," which took place about 1600 to 1900. The range between these extremes is much smaller than the range defined by warming over the past 100 years.

⑦ According to the National Climatic Data Center, the average rate of global temperature increase since 1976 has been about 5.4 Fahrenheit degrees (3 Celsius degrees) per century. By comparison, the world has warmed by 5 to 9 Fahrenheit degrees (2.8 to 5 Celsius degrees) since the depths of the last ice age, 18,000 to 20,000 years ago....

Analytical Writing Models

Harmless Media Images
by Anthony Simpson

After examining the issues surrounding the media and self-image, I agree wholeheartedly that the media are not responsible for teens' body images. Therefore media images should not be regulated and be restricted for teenagers.

One reason I maintain this position is that the media often show healthy images. In the article "The Ugly Effects of Beauty," Marcus Cano presents compelling data regarding the positive effect of media images. For example, the editor of *Men's Health* explains that his magazine shows what fit men look like (Cano 57).

Critics of these images tend to point out that they make boys take extreme measures (Cano 56). However, to subscribe to the notion that media images damage boys' health is unfounded. Studies actually demonstrate that only 2 percent of boys use steroids (Allegre 28).

I am also opposed to regulating media images due to teens' knowledge that the images are not real. Pedro Gutierrez emphasizes in his essay, "The Image Artist," that retouching creates ideal images to sell products (Gutierrez 60). One particularly convincing statistic is that female models typically "weigh 23 percent less than the average woman" (Cano 55).

Whether media images harm teens will no doubt remain a controversial issue. After reviewing relevant data and reflecting on my own experiences as an adolescent, I still contend that the media cannot be held accountable for teens' self-images.

Global Warming
by Sir John Houghton

The term "global warming" is used by the general public to refer to the phenomenon of global change arising from human activities that result in an increase in greenhouse gases, notably carbon dioxide, in the atmosphere. One manifestation of this climate change is the observed rise in global mean temperature at Earth's surface. This climate change involves much more than just increases in global temperatures, however. Changes in precipitation, drought, and water resources, for instance, are also involved. Such factors can have a profound impact on the environment and human endeavors.

The increase in temperatures cannot be entirely explained by natural cycles. It is largely the result of human activities. Chief among these activities is the burning of fossil fuels, which include coal, oil, and gasoline. When these fuels are burned, they release gases that act like the glass in a greenhouse. They trap heat in Earth's atmosphere. These gases — which include water vapor, carbon dioxide, and methane — are called greenhouse gases.

These gases enhance the natural "greenhouse effect." This effect was recognized about 200 years ago and keeps Earth's surface about 36 Fahrenheit degrees (20 Celsius degrees) warmer than it would otherwise be.

The greenhouse effect scarcely changed for thousands of years. This was because the levels of greenhouse gases remained stable. However, one of these gases, carbon dioxide, started a dramatic increase in the 1800s. The increase was due to the burning of large amounts of fossil fuels during the Industrial Revolution. Since then, the burning of fossil fuels has increased. More greenhouse gases have entered the atmosphere, and temperatures have continued to rise. There is some debate as to how much of climate change is caused by humans. Some people who doubt that human activities cause global warming say that climate changes could be due to changes in the Sun's output. But in 2007 a study revealed that the Sun's output has been decreasing since 1985, even though global temperatures have been rising ever faster.

Gathering Evidence

It is common for temperature and climate trends to change for natural reasons — that is, for reasons that have nothing to do with human activities. Natural reasons are not enough to explain global warming, however. Natural climate cycles tend to unfold slowly, but the changes seen with global warming are relatively sudden.

Over the past 1,000 years, temperature changes have fit within a range defined by two extreme periods: a warm period, which took place about 1200 to 1400, and a "little ice age," which took place about 1600 to 1900. The range between these extremes is much smaller than the range defined by warming over the past 100 years.

According to the National Climatic Data Center, the average rate of global temperature increase since 1976 has been about 5.4 Fahrenheit degrees (3 Celsius degrees) per century. By comparison, the world has warmed by 5 to 9 Fahrenheit degrees (2.8 to 5 Celsius degrees) since the depths of the last ice age, 18,000 to 20,000 years ago....

Assessing Research and Arguments

For the Teacher

Defining the Strategy

The three types of analytical academic writing are argument, informative/ explanatory, and narrative. In particular, the Common Core State Standards place specific emphasis on writing and evaluating arguments. Learning to write strong, compelling, and well-supported arguments can be a challenge, but by being able to effectively assess research and arguments, students become more able to write exemplary arguments of their own.

A solid *argument* puts forth a claim that is supported by one or more credible or persuasive reasons. A solid *claim* is one that is supported with compelling reasons. In addition, concrete, relevant *evidence* is necessary to support each reason. This evidence can come in the form of details, examples, or data. When assessing an argument, you evaluate whether the claims made are supported with valid reasoning and relevant and sufficient evidence. These components are crucial to a solid argument. Without them, an argument is invalid.

Research, in and of itself, always involves argument writing. Beyond relating facts that are already known, research involves asking questions and developing ideas based on an examination of facts. It includes not only the discovery of facts, but interpretations of those facts and revision of the ideas and theories based on those facts. Therefore, assessments of research and arguments are complementary, and equally vital.

Assessment, of course, requires analytical thinking, which increases the rigor required of student thinking. Moreover, the assessment of research and arguments fits within Quadrants C on the Rigor/Relevance Framework. This activity is also useful any time students embark on assignments that include research. They will be able to use their assessment skills to evaluate the information and data they encounter and decide its validity and usefulness in their own writing projects. Additionally, students may use this strategy to examine arguments, in their own writing and in the writing of others.

Applying the Strategy

Standards 1, 8, and 9 of the Common Core State Standards College and Career Anchor Standards for Writing are all relevant to this writing strategy. Standard 1 focuses on the writing of arguments to support claims and the analysis of substantive topics or texts, using valid reasoning and relevant sufficient evidence. In order to write an argument, one must first be able to evaluate and assess an argument to understand the characteristics of an argument and how they function together.

Anchor standard 8 covers gathering relevant information from multiple print and digital sources and assessing the credibility of each source. Assessing the credibility of sources, of course, is a key skill that all students must develop to become successful writers of research and arguments. Any time students are gathering information for their writing, the assessment of research and arguments should be a main writing strategy used.

Anchor standard 9 requires students to draw evidence from literary or informational texts to support analysis, reflection, and research. This writing strategy can be used to help students assess the evidence they find in informational texts and determine how it supports their research.

Assessing research and arguments constitutes an effective strategy in middle and secondary programs across most content areas. Throughout middle school and secondary school, students are asked to engage in many different types of research projects.

Middle School

- Science
  - ○ the assessment of research and evidence to support scientific claims
- Social Studies
  - ○ understanding of fact and opinion
  - ○ primary and secondary sources
- Math
  - ○ constructing mathematical arguments and reasoning to support algorithms
- ELA
  - ○ supporting claims with logical reasoning and relevant evidence
  - ○ developing topics with relevant facts

Secondary School

- Science
  - ○ the assessment of research and evidence to support scientific claims
- Social Studies
  - ○ assessing the strengths and limitations of historical sources
- Math
  - ○ understanding and creating geometric proofs
- ELA
  - ○ supporting claims with logical reasoning and relevant evidence
  - ○ developing topics with relevant facts

Common Core State Standards

College and Career Readiness Anchor Standards for Writing

Text Types and Purposes

1. Write arguments to support claims in an analysis of substantive topics or texts, using valid reasoning and relevant and sufficient evidence.

2. Write informative/explanatory texts to examine and convey complex ideas and information both clearly and accurately through the effective selection, organization, and analysis of content.

Production and Distribution of Writing

4. Produce clear and coherent writing in which the development, organization, and style are appropriate to task, purpose, and audience.

5. Develop and strengthen writing as needed by planning, revising, editing, rewriting, or trying a new approach.

Research to Build and Present Knowledge

8. Gather relevant information from multiple print and digital sources, assess the credibility and accuracy of each source, and integrate the information while avoiding plagiarism.

Teaching the Strategy

Introduce the strategy by reviewing the three types of claims typically seen in an argument:

- **Substantiation.** This is a claim that something is a fact. The claim tries to prove that something exists or is truthful. *Increasing temperatures are not the cause of the polar ice melt.*

- **Evaluation.** This is a claim of value. It argues that one thing is better or worse than another thing. *A democracy is a better system of government than a monarchy.*

- **Recommendation.** This is a claim that calls for a specific action. *We should form a committee to improve the safety of our playgrounds.*

When assessing an argument the following pieces should be analyzed:

- the claim
- reasons and evidence
- citations
- counterclaims
- the conclusion

Tools that can aid in the assessment of research and argument include rubrics and checklists.

- **Rubric.** A rubric is a document — often a table or chart — that lists the criteria for an assignment, in this case, a piece of writing. The rubric for a particular writing assignment should be shared before the assignment to establish expectations for students. A rubric should also determine the various levels of mastery and provide clear descriptors to determine what level a writer has achieved for each expectation.

Criteria	Insufficient 1	Developing 2	Sufficient 3	Exemplary 4	Score
The introduction clearly states the writer's claim, or thesis statement	Needs a topic sentence that states the writer's claim	Includes the writer's claim, but it is unclear	Topic sentence clearly states the writer's claim	Compelling topic sentence clearly states the writer's claim	
Strong reasons and evidence support the writer's claim.	Needs supporting reasons and evidence	Includes reason(s) or evidence that are not convincing or relevant	Includes at least two convincing reasons and textual evidence	Includes three or more convincing reasons and textual evidence	
The writer includes a counterclaim and response.	Needs a counterclaim and response	Includes one counterclaim, but there is no response, or the response is unrelated	Includes at least one counterclaim and response with strong evidence	Includes two counterclaims and responses with strong evidence	
The writer includes citation information for textual evidence.	No textual evidence or citation information	One or two pieces of textual evidence with incorrect citation information	Two or more pieces of textual evidence with correct citation information	Various textual evidence (paraphrased/quoted) with correct citation information	

Criteria	Insufficient 1	Developing 2	Sufficient 3	Exemplary 4	Score
Transitions introduce reasons and evidence.	Needs transition words or phrases	One or two transition words or phrases that introduce reasons and evidence	Three or more transition words or phrases that introduce reasons and evidence	Variety of transition words or phrases effectively introduce reasons and evidence	
The conclusion restates a thesis and offers a recommendation.	Needs a recommendation or recommendation is off-topic	Offers a recommendation but it is not meaningful or actionable	Offers a recommendation related to the thesis	Offers a meaningful and actionable recommendation	
The writing follows conventions of mechanics, spelling, and usage.	Errors in grammar, spelling, punctuation, and capitalization that impede reader understanding	Some errors in grammar, spelling, punctuation, and capitalization	Few errors in grammar, spelling, punctuation, and capitalization	Correct grammar, spelling, punctuation, and capitalization	
				Overall Score	

- **Scoring Guide.** A scoring guide can be used to self- or peer-assess a piece of writing. It focuses on key elements and guides revision.

Self-Assessment/Peer Assessment

		1	2	3	4
1. Does the introduction clearly identify the research topic?	Self	1	2	3	4
	Partner	1	2	3	4
2. Does a claim or a focus/thesis statement state the plan for the paper?	Self	1	2	3	4
	Partner	1	2	3	4
3. Do facts and evidence from multiple sources support the claim or focus/thesis statement?	Self	1	2	3	4
	Partner	1	2	3	4
4. Is there a counterclaim and response with relevant evidence?	Self	1	2	3	4
	Partner	1	2	3	4
5. Does the paper include quotes and citations from multiple texts?	Self	1	2	3	4
	Partner	1	2	3	4
6. Are there precise words and transition words or phrases	Self	1	2	3	4
	Partner	1	2	3	4
7. Does the conclusion restate the claim or focus/thesis statement and add a final thought or recommendation?	Self	1	2	3	4
	Partner	1	2	3	4
8. Does the paper follow conventions of grammar, usage, mechanics, and spelling?	Self	1	2	3	4
	Partner	1	2	3	4

*Rating Scale
① = Insufficient   ② = Developing   ③ = Sufficient   ④ = Exemplary

- **Checklist.** A checklist asks yes-or-no questions to evaluate information. Checklists are useful for identifying reliable sources. The checklist below can be used for both print and digital sources.

Title: _____

Source/Website URL: _____

Publisher: _____

	Yes	No
Does the source relate to my topic?	☐	☐
Is the publisher reliable?	☐	☐
Does the purpose of the source meet my needs?	☐	☐
Does the source contain too much general information?	☐	☐
Does the source contain specific facts related to my topic?	☐	☐
Is the information well researched?	☐	☐
Are there errors in spelling, grammar, or punctuation?	☐	☐
Is the source current, or has it recently been updated?	☐	☐
For websites: Does the website link to other reliable sites?	☐	☐

How would you rate this source? Circle your answer.

Excellent   Good   Fair   Poor

How would you rate your search? Circle your answer.

Excellent   Good   Fair   Poor

This source is not useful for _____

_____

_____

_____

Directed Writing Activity

1. This activity requires students to read and assess an argument. They will assess the writing for valid reasons and sufficient evidence. Additionally, they will assess the credibility and accuracy of the sources.

2. As appropriate to your class, copy and distribute either the essay "Dr. King's Revolution Continues Today" or another applicable sample argument.

3. Ask students to read the argument one time without making any notes. Then have them read it a second time and identify the following by marking the text: the claim, reasons and evidence, citations, counterclaims, and the conclusion.

4. As a class, complete the rubric for the argument. Discuss with students the score they would give the writing for each criteria and why. Encourage them to cite information and evidence in the writing to support their opinion.

5. Next, search online for information about Dr. Martin Luther King, Jr. Choose two or three websites to evaluate with students. Decide which has the most reliable information and discuss the reasons for this.

6. Assign the independent writing activity.

Sample Rubric

Criteria	Insufficient 1	Developing 2	Sufficient 3	Exemplary 4	Score
The introduction clearly states the writer's claim, or thesis statement	Needs a topic sentence that states the writer's claim	Includes the writer's claim, but it is unclear	Topic sentence clearly states the writer's claim	Compelling topic sentence clearly states the writer's claim	4
Strong reasons and evidence support the writer's claim.	Needs supporting reasons and evidence	Includes reason(s) or evidence that are not convincing or relevant	Includes at least two convincing reasons and textual evidence	Includes three or more convincing reasons and textual evidence	3
The writer includes a counterclaim and response.	Needs a counterclaim and response	Includes one counterclaim, but there is no response, or the response is unrelated	Includes at least one counterclaim and response with strong evidence	Includes two counterclaims and responses with strong evidence	3
The writer includes citation information for textual evidence.	No textual evidence or citation information	One or two pieces of textual evidence with incorrect citation information	Two or more pieces of textual evidence with correct citation information	Various textual evidence (paraphrased/quoted) with correct citation information	4

Sample Rubric (Continued)

Criteria	Insufficient 1	Developing 2	Sufficient 3	Exemplary 4	Score
Transitions introduce reasons and evidence.	Needs transition words or phrases	One or two transition words or phrases that introduce reasons and evidence	Three or more transition words or phrases that introduce reasons and evidence	Variety of transition words or phrases effectively introduce reasons and evidence	4
The conclusion restates a thesis and offers a recommendation.	Needs a recommendation or recommendation is off-topic	Offers a recommendation but it is not meaningful or actionable	Offers a recommendation related to the thesis	Offers a meaningful and actionable recommendation	4
The writing follows conventions of mechanics, spelling, and usage.	Errors in grammar, spelling, punctuation, and capitalization that impede reader understanding	Some errors in grammar, spelling, punctuation, and capitalization	Few errors in grammar, spelling, punctuation, and capitalization	Correct grammar, spelling, punctuation, and capitalization	4
				Overall Score	26

References

Rigor and Research, Building Writing Proficiency in the Content Areas. New York: Scholastic Achievement Partners, 2012.

Writing Arguments and Conducting Research. New York: Scholastic, 2012.

For the Student

Independent Writing Activity

Follow these directions to practice assessing research and arguments.

1. Choose an argument paper to evaluate. Identify the following aspects of the paper:

   - the claim

   - reasons and evidence

   - citations, counterclaims

   - the conclusion

2. Use an assessment rubric to assess the argument. Then imagine it was written by one of your peers and complete a peer assessment of the writing.

3. Write a brief summary of your opinion of how well the author presented his or her argument. Which evidence was most compelling? Was the claim supported? Were the resources cited reliable?

_____

_____

_____

_____

_____

_____

_____

_____

4. Exchange the paper you assessed with a partner. Assess each other's papers. Then discuss and compare your assessments.

Argument Paper

Dr. King's Revolution Continues Today

by Lea Santana

After reading "I Have a Dream" by Martin Luther King, Jr., I am convinced that his statement "The whirlwinds of revolt will continue to shake the foundations of our nation until the bright day of justice emerges" still rings true today.

When King spoke of a "sweltering summer of discontent," he was writing 50 years ago. Today, many Americans are still dissatisfied, and they have formed protest movements across the country. The Tea Party and the Occupy movements are two examples. The Occupy protesters demonstrating in many cities are revolting against a number of perceived injustices, from the cost of a college education to government's failure to punish Wall Street executives (Kleinfeld 59).

King described a "lonely island of poverty in the midst of a vast ocean of prosperity." The divide between rich and poor is even greater now. Incomes for 90 percent of Americans have been stagnant for a generation or more, while the wealthiest 10 percent have seen their incomes rise astronomically. The wealthiest 1 percent have done the best, improving their incomes by 33 percent in just two decades (Vasquez 11).

People may say that King was speaking of racial disparities, and that today's situation is not parallel, but I disagree. King spent the final years of his life working for economic justice (Garrow 24). Therefore, I think he would say that the "bright day of justice" is not here yet as long as such imbalanced economic divisions still exist.

To conclude, the current economic conditions have created an atmosphere of uncertainty, and many citizens are displeased with the status quo. I maintain that Martin Luther King, Jr., would urge us all to continue with the "whirlwinds of revolt" he helped to start. I, too, believe we should never stop protesting against economic and social inequality, until we achieve true justice for all.

Rubric

Rubric

Criteria	Insufficient 1	Developing 2	Sufficient 3	Exemplary 4	Score
The introduction clearly states the writer's claim, or thesis statement	Needs a topic sentence that states the writer's claim	Includes the writer's claim, but it is unclear	Topic sentence clearly states the writer's claim	Compelling topic sentence clearly states the writer's claim	
Strong reasons and evidence support the writer's claim.	Needs supporting reasons and evidence	Includes reason(s) or evidence that are not convincing or relevant	Includes at least two convincing reasons and textual evidence	Includes three or more convincing reasons and textual evidence	
The writer includes a counterclaim and response.	Needs a counterclaim and response	Includes one counterclaim, but there is no response, or the response is unrelated	Includes at least one counterclaim and response with strong evidence	Includes two counterclaims and responses with strong evidence	
The writer includes citation information for textual evidence.	No textual evidence or citation information	One or two pieces of textual evidence with incorrect citation information	Two or more pieces of textual evidence with correct citation information	Various textual evidence (paraphrased/ quoted) with correct citation information	

Rubric (Continued)

Criteria	Insufficient 1	Developing 2	Sufficient 3	Exemplary 4	Score
Transitions introduce reasons and evidence.	Needs transition words or phrases	One or two transition words or phrases that introduce reasons and evidence	Three or more transition words or phrases that introduce reasons and evidence	Variety of transition words or phrases effectively introduce reasons and evidence	
The conclusion restates a thesis and offers a recommendation.	Needs a recommendation or recommendation is off-topic	Offers a recommendation but it is not meaningful or actionable	Offers a recommendation related to the thesis	Offers a meaningful and actionable recommendation	
The writing follows conventions of mechanics, spelling, and usage.	Errors in grammar, spelling, punctuation, and capitalization that impede reader understanding	Some errors in grammar, spelling, punctuation, and capitalization	Few errors in grammar, spelling, punctuation, and capitalization	Correct grammar, spelling, punctuation, and capitalization	
				Overall Score	

Self-Assessment/Peer Assessment

1. Does the introduction clearly identify the research topic?	Self	1	2	3	4
	Partner	1	2	3	4
2. Does a claim or a focus/thesis statement state the plan for the paper?	Self	1	2	3	4
	Partner	1	2	3	4
3. Do facts and evidence from multiple sources support the claim or focus/thesis statement?	Self	1	2	3	4
	Partner	1	2	3	4
4. Is there a counterclaim and response with relevant evidence?	Self	1	2	3	4
	Partner	1	2	3	4
5. Does the paper include quotes and citations from multiple texts?	Self	1	2	3	4
	Partner	1	2	3	4
6. Are there precise words and transition words or phrases?	Self	1	2	3	4
	Partner	1	2	3	4
7. Does the conclusion restate the claim or focus/thesis statement and add a final thought or recommendation?	Self	1	2	3	4
	Partner	1	2	3	4
8. Does the paper follow conventions of grammar, usage, mechanics, and spelling?	Self	1	2	3	4
	Partner	1	2	3	4

*Rating Scale
① = Insufficient   ② = Developing   ③ = Sufficient   ④ = Exemplary

■ Citing Evidence from the Text

Defining the Strategy

Technology has made the world our oyster when it comes to finding information. With a few quick clicks of a mouse, we can easily find a wealth of information about a variety of topics. This information that we draw from literary or informational texts can be used to support our analysis, reflection, and research. When we use the thoughts or ideas of others in our own research, we are citing evidence. Citing evidence makes our own work more credible because it helps the audience determine, more easily, how and why we come to our conclusions.

While we should use evidence to support our own analysis and research, more importantly, we must credit sources of information used within our own work. The Internet has made a vast amount of knowledge more easily accessible; however, with this great resource has also come a greater responsibility to respect and protect intellectual and creative property. Plagiarism is a serious offense with serious consequences. According to the *Merriam-Webster's Collegiate Dictionary*, *plagiarize* means "to commit literary theft" and to "present as new and original an idea or product derived from an existing source." For students, failing to cite evidence correctly may lead to a failing grade or expulsion from school. For professionals, it may lead to job loss, banning from a profession, or legal action. Teaching our students to be responsible and courteous researchers is a lifelong skill that will aid them in their ongoing educational and professional lives.

The main objective of citing evidence from the text is to reflect on, analyze, draw conclusions about, justify, synthesize, and/or evaluate information. These processes add rigor and relevance to the learning of students because they require students to make connections among ideas from a number of sources on an authentic subject and then relate those connections to their own prior knowledge of the topic. This overall process solidly fits within Quadrant D on the Rigor/Relevance Framework.

Applying the Strategy

Teaching students to cite evidence from the text is an effective strategy in most content areas and in middle and secondary programs.

Middle School

- Science
  - researching ways to increase garden productivity
- Social Studies
  - researching challenges for immigrants in the United States
- Math
  - researching ways that natural disasters have changed building shape/design
- ELA
  - researching forms of shorthand used in electronic communications

Secondary School

- Science
  - researching most practical alternative energy solutions

- Social Studies
  - researching ways in which wars have affected government policy
- Math
  - researching ways that math has played a role in secret codes
- ELA
  - researching the effects of a time period on a piece of literature or writer

Common Core State Standards

College and Career Readiness Anchor Standards for Writing

Research to Build and Present Knowledge

7. Conduct short as well as more sustained research projects based on focused questions, demonstrating understanding of the subject under investigation.

8. Gather relevant information from multiple print and digital sources, assess the credibility and accuracy of each source, and integrate the information while avoiding plagiarism.

9. Draw evidence from literary or informational texts to support analysis, reflection, and research.

Teaching the Strategy

Introduce the strategy by explaining that citing evidence from the text is used to do the following:

- **Avoid plagiarism**. You must credit ideas or thoughts that are not your own to avoid serious consequences.

- **Allow readers to find sources.** You add authenticity to your work when you include your sources. Readers can seek out these sources to learn more about the topic or assess the credibility and accuracy of a source.
- **Add credibility.** Your list of sources allows readers to see that you have considered the opinion of others and sought authoritative information to develop your ideas and thoughts. Often your research helps you answer a question or solve a problem. By synthesizing multiple sources on the subject, you demonstrate your understanding of the subject under research.

Explain that citing evidence can take many forms in your work, including a quotation, paraphrase, or summary. Reinforce that an effective researcher is selective in choosing which information to incorporate in his or her work and avoids overreliance on any one source of information.

- **Quotation.** You may choose to quote someone's words directly if they are so eloquent or so powerful that paraphrasing or summarizing the ideas might lose effect. This technique should be used more sparingly than paraphrasing or summarizing.

    Example: In *The Old Man and the Sea*, Ernest Hemingway writes, "A man can be destroyed but not defeated" (103). Although the old man is physically crippled from exhaustion and the lack of food and water, he still does not give up hope that he can bring in the big fish. His spirit and faith stay strong despite his failures and setbacks.

- **Paraphrasing.** You may paraphrase much of the evidence that you cite in your own work by putting an idea from a source into your own words.

    Example: In *The Old Man and the Sea*, Santiago was characterized as appearing almost emaciated and very weathered from the many days at sea. The only physical part that still appeared young was his eyes (Hemingway 9–10). This description aptly shows that even at the beginning of the man's journey, he is already physically weaker than the younger fishermen. The fact that his eyes still appear young is important: as eyes are often considered to show the feelings or state of being of a person, the reader concludes that the old man is still confident and resolute in his goal to catch a fish.

- **Summarizing.** You may also choose to use a larger section of a person's book, paper, or website as evidence by focusing on the main ideas and concisely restating them in a few sentences.

    Example: Toward the end of *The Old Man and the Sea*, Santiago regrets killing the fish. He feels as if he has somehow disrespected it (Hemingway 105–115). Although Santiago seems to temporarily reach his goal, the reader comes to understand that the goal is not only about catching the fish but also about honoring and respecting the greatness of his opponent. Santiago's dream of catching such an honorable beast is mutilated along with the fish.

Teach that citing evidence from the text — whether it comes in the form of a quote, paraphrase, or summary — requires you to use a standard format for citation in order to identify a source correctly and communicate efficiently with your audience. Many professions and subject areas have their own way of citing evidence and documenting sources. These include the following:

- **APA:** used in psychology, nursing, education, and other social sciences
- **MLA:** used in literature, arts, and humanities
- **Chicago:** used in history and all subjects
- **Turabian:** used for all subjects
- **Other:** additional styles for life sciences, health sciences, law, government resources, engineering, and social sciences

Teachers often choose the format that is generally taught at the school, most of the time in a student's ELA or English class. Most often this is MLA style. More detailed information about MLA format can be found in the *MLA Handbook for Writers of Research Papers* or online at http://www.mla.org. Emphasize that while learning a standard format may seem daunting, it is important to the process of becoming a competent researcher and communicator. Most formats require citation within the text as well as within a Bibliography/Works Cited page.

Note that all three samples listed above use MLA format. Reviewing these samples, you will also discover that citing evidence often involves four components:

- **Introduce the source of information.** The introduction may be a phrase followed by a comma or a full sentence followed by a colon. Often the introduction lists the title of the source, the author of the source, or both. However, this information does not necessarily have to come at the beginning of the sentence or even at all. The introduction may also provide context for readers to prepare them for the information.

- **Quote, paraphrase, or summarize the information.**

- **Cite the location of the information.** This information is found in parentheses after the cited information. Note that for printed sources, this includes the author's last name and page number on which the information can be found. Note that the author's name is not needed if it is stated in the introduction. In addition, if you want to summarize an entire work, you only need to list the author's name, either in the introduction or in the parentheses. For non-print sources, you might not have a page number but rather a section number or paragraph number. For a web publication that contains no pagination or other type of reference markers, you should only include the author's name either in the introduction or in parentheses, or a shortened version of the title if a person is not identified.

- **Explain, analyze, reflect, evaluate, synthesize, or draw conclusions about the information.**

Clarify that citing evidence mostly takes place during the prewriting and drafting stages of the writing process. These are the steps in which writers gather information, develop ideas, and support their thoughts. Caution students not to wait until the revising or editing stages to add in citations, as this may inadvertently lead to errors.

Directed Writing Activity

As the MLA format is one of the most common citation formats taught in middle schools and high schools, it will be the citation format used in the following activity.

This activity will require students to gather relevant information from a source and integrate information into a text while avoiding plagiarism. Have students read the article "Teen sleep: Why is your teen so tired?" about teen sleep from the following link.

http://www.mayoclinic.com/health/teens-health/CC00019

1. Explain to the class that you are using the article to support an essay with the thesis statement "Later school start times are beneficial to both students and teachers." Ask students to identify relevant information from the source to support your thesis. As a class, discuss which information would be best to quote, paraphrase, or summarize.

2. With students, fill out the Source Chart document with information from the text. Have students guide you with suggestions for paraphrasing or summarizing portions of the text and identify each piece of information as such in the second column.

3. As a class, complete the third column by adding the correct citation information in parentheses. Example: (Mayo Clinic 1). Then discuss how each piece of information supports the thesis by explaining, reflecting on, analyzing, synthesizing, and drawing conclusions about the information. In the fourth column of the Source Chart, record students' thoughts and ideas.

4. Practice with students to create a Works Cited page entry for the article. Sample:

   Mayo Clinic staff. "Teen Sleep: Why is your teen so tired?" *The Mayo Clinic*. Mayo Foundation for Medical Education and Research, 4 Aug. 2011. Web. 15 April 2012.

5. Using the Source Chart, have students write a paragraph that supports the thesis and incorporates evidence from the text. Urge students to consider their development, organization, and

style. Remind students to include the following: topic sentence, introduction of the evidence, evidence, citation, reflection and/or analysis, and concluding sentence.

6. After students complete their paragraphs, review and discuss the assignment. Encourage students to share their paragraphs and explain how they integrated source information effectively to avoid plagiarism and to support the thesis. Review how the citations and the Works Cited entry work together to communicate to the reader.

7. Assign the independent writing activity.

Reference

InTASC Model Core Teaching Standards: A Resource for State Dialogue.

For the Student

Independent Writing Activity

Follow these directions to write an essay about the effects of social media on teenagers. Gather relevant information from the sources below, integrate information into the text, and follow a standard format for citation. Be sure the development, organization, and style are appropriate to task, purpose, and audience.

1. Read and analyze the following sources about the impact of social media on teenagers.

   • http://pediatrics.aappublications.org/content/127/4/800.full

   • http://www.apa.org/news/press/releases/2011/08/social-kids.aspx

   • http://www.californiateenhealth.org/wp-content/uploads/2011/09/SocialMediaAug2011.pdf

2. Develop an opinion about the effects of social media on teenagers. For example, does it have more of a positive impact or more of a negative impact on teenagers? How would you describe the impact on teenage life? Write your thesis statement below.

   _____

   _____

   _____

   _____

3. Gather important information from your sources that support your opinion. Make decisions about which information should be quoted, paraphrased, or summarized. Use the Source Chart or an outline to organize your information and ideas for your essay.

4. Write an essay about the effects of social media on teenagers. Remember to include an introduction and a conclusion.

5. In the following space, create Works Cited entries for the three sources. Review the MLA Handbook for Writers of Research Papers or www.mla.org for examples of Works Cited entries.

Works Cited

Source Chart

Source Chart					
Thesis Statement: _____					
Paragraph #: _____	Topic Sentence: _____				
	Explanations, Reflections, Analysis, Conclusions				
	Source Information				
	Paraphrase, Summary, or Quote				
	Information				

Comparison-and-Contrast Writing

To the Teacher

Defining the Strategy

It has been said that one of the best ways to learn about lions is to analyze cats. Observing the similarities and the differences can help us learn more about each. In comparison-and-contrast writing, learners identify and analyze the similarities and differences among objects, ideas, people, and events. They will then organize and present their findings in writing, a process which further enhances the learner's opportunity to examine and convey complex ideas and information through the effective selection, organization, and analysis of content. A comparison-and-contrast essay or article also requires them to use language skills, to think clearly, and to define and express ideas through clear and coherent writing in which the development, organization, and style are appropriate to the task and purpose.

The objective of comparison-and-contrast writing is to increase the writer's level of rigorous and relevant thinking. It requires learners to think in complex ways and to apply the knowledge and skills that they have learned. Comparison-and-contrast writing fits solidly within Quadrant D on the Rigor/Relevance Framework.

Applying the Strategy

Across most content areas and in middle and secondary programs, comparison-and-contrast writing is an effective strategy.

Middle School

- Science
  - comparing climate zones and habitats, geologic eras, elements and compounds, scientific theories and laws
- Social Studies
  - comparing historic events and time periods, famous people, political and economic systems
- Math
  - comparing demographic trends, mathematical processes, sets
- ELA
  - comparing genres, opinions, themes, characters, the use of figurative language

Secondary School

- Science
  - comparing chemical reactions, atomic structures, responses to climate change
- Social Studies
  - comparing current events and historic events, economic systems, consequences of economic choices
- Math
  - comparing the significance of sample sizes, mathematical solutions and methods, changes in inflation and growth patterns over time
- ELA
  - comparing genres, arguments, points of view, tone and mood, dramatic interpretations, books and poems

Common Core State Standards

College and Career Readiness Anchor Standards for Writing

Text Types and Purposes

2. Write informative/explanatory texts to examine and convey complex ideas and information clearly and accurately through the effective selection, organization, and analysis of content.

Production and Distribution of Writing

4. Produce clear and coherent writing in which the development, organization, and style are appropriate to task, purpose, and audience.

5. Develop and strengthen writing as needed by planning, revising, editing, rewriting, or trying a new approach.

Teaching the Strategy

Introduce the strategy by explaining that comparison-and-contrast writing is often used for two main purposes:

- **To explain.** Comparison-and-contrast writing can be used to explain why something happened, why a decision was reached, or what an idea means. For example, comparison-and-contrast writing might be used to explain why President Truman chose to drop the atomic bomb on Hiroshima rather than to invade Japan as a way to end the war in the Pacific.

- **To evaluate.** Comparison-and-contrast writing can be used to tell why one idea, thing, or solution is better suited than another for a particular purpose. For example, a comparison-contrast essay might be written to show why algae produce a better biofuel than corn.

Writing a comparison-contrast essay or article requires a careful analysis of two or more subjects to determine how they are alike and different. Often, graphic organizers are useful in recording, recognizing, and developing these similarities and differences. Two commonly used graphic organizers are:

- **Venn diagram.** A Venn diagram is a graphic organizer that makes a graphic representation of features or details. It shows at a glance the key parts of the whole and their relations, helping the learner to comprehend texts and solve problems. Venn diagrams are useful for comparing and contrasting two items that share common characteristics or attributes. A Venn diagram consists of two or sometimes three or more overlapping circles. Each circle represents one of the subjects being compared. The space where the circles overlap shows the similarities between the subjects. The spaces outside the overlapping area show how the subjects are different. Venn diagrams work particularly well in math and English. For example, a Venn diagram can show the similarities of different geometric shapes or the similarities and differences between characters in a play.

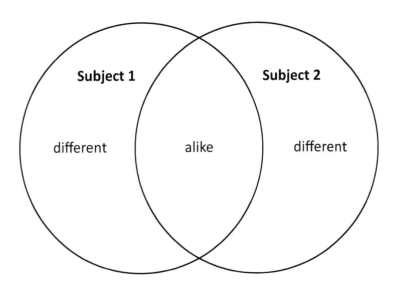

- **Comparison-and-contrast matrix.** A comparison-and-contrast matrix organizes ideas and details in a way similar to a Venn diagram, but it is more easily expandable and allows more space for adding details about a complex relationship. A matrix, for example, is well-suited to comparing and contrasting a complex topic such as the lead characters in Shakespeare's *Romeo and Juliet*.

	Item 1	Item 2
Characteristic 1		
Characteristic 2		
Characteristic 3		

Comparison-contrast writing is typically organized in one of three ways:

- **Subject-by-subject.** The first idea, topic, or event is fully discussed. Then the writer discusses the second subject while pointing out how it is similar to or different from the first subject.
- **Point-by-point.** The two subjects are compared using a few details at a time.
- **Similarities-to-differences.** The writer describes how the two subjects are alike and then describes how they are different.

Directed Writing Activity

1. This activity will require students to produce clear and coherent writing in which development, organization, and style are appropriate to task and purpose. Choose two objects, ideas, people, or events for students to compare. Students should know the subjects well enough to write a couple of paragraphs about them without needing to do additional research. The subjects must share enough similarities and differences for the comparison to be meaningful. For example, they might compare bicycles and cars, high school and middle school, or dogs and cats.

2. As appropriate to your class and the topic, copy and distribute either the Venn diagram form or the comparison-and-contrast form to students, or allow them to choose one and create it themselves.

3. Ask students to think carefully about the topic and list similarities and differences on their graphic organizers.

4. Develop a class organizer with students' help. Have students guide you in labeling it correctly.

5. Discuss the similarities between the two subjects. Invite students to share points from their own organizers, and add these points to the class organizer.

6. Discuss differences between the two subjects, and enter ideas in the appropriate portion of the organizer.

7. Remind students of the three methods for organizing comparison-contrast writing. Review, as necessary, the components of an essay, including the introduction and conclusion. Then instruct students to write a two- or three-paragraph essay comparing their subjects. Urge them to consider how the development, organization, and style of their writing is appropriate to its purpose.

8. After learners complete their essays, review and discuss the assignment. Encourage students to describe the organizers they used and why they chose them. Ask students how they organized their essays and to explain their choices. Invite students to consider what they would do differently if given this assignment again.

9. Assign the independent writing activity.

Sample Organizer

Bicycles and Cars

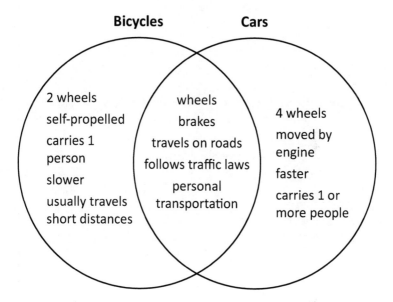

Bicycles

Cars

2 wheels
self-propelled
carries 1 person
slower
usually travels short distances

wheels
brakes
travels on roads
follows traffic laws
personal transportation

4 wheels
moved by engine
faster
carries 1 or more people

Reference

Marzano, R., et al. *Classroom Instruction That Works*. Alexandria, VA: ASCD, 2001.

For the Student

Independent Writing Activity

Follow these directions to write a compare-contrast essay. Develop your writing appropriately by planning, revising, and editing.

1. Choose two objects, ideas, people, or events that you know well and write a comparison-and-contrast essay. Here are some topic suggestions:

   • a face-to-face conversation and a cell phone conversation

   • robots and people

   • young children and teenagers

   • horror movies and comedies

   • walking to school and riding a bus to school

2. Identify your purpose for writing. Will you write to explain, to evaluate, or something else?

   _____

3. Complete a graphic organizer showing points of similarity and difference.

4. Choose a method of organizing your essay. Will you use point-by-point, subject-by-subject, or similarity-to-difference organization?

   _____

5. Write a compare-contrast essay about your topic. Remember to include an introduction and a conclusion.

Sample Comparison-and-Contrast Matrix

Cell Phone Conversation and Face-to-Face Conversation

	Cell-Phone Conversation	Face-to-Face Conversation
Gestures	If gestures are used, they are not seen by other party.	Gestures can be used and contribute to communication between the parties.
Eye contact	The parties cannot make eye contact.	Automatic eye contact can contribute to understanding.
Use of words	Words are the main means of communicating.	Words are the main means of communication, but gestures, tone, eye contact, and other elements can add to meaning of words.
Give and take	Both parties can speak and listen, can give and take equally during the conversation.	Both parties can speak and listen, give and take equally during the conversation.
Tone of voice	Tone of voice can be used to convey feelings and attitude.	Tone of voice can be used to convey feelings and attitude.
Distance between speakers	Parties can speak at any distance from one another.	Parties must be close together to communicate.

Sample Venn Diagram

Comparing and Contrasting Robots and People

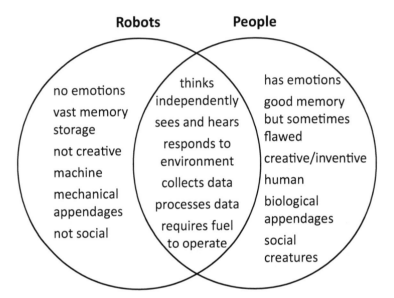

Robots

People

no emotions

vast memory storage

not creative

machine

mechanical appendages

not social

thinks independently

sees and hears

responds to environment

collects data

processes data

requires fuel to operate

has emotions

good memory but sometimes flawed

creative/inventive

human

biological appendages

social creatures

Comparison-Contrast Matrix

	Item 1	Item 2
Characteristic 1		
Characteristic 2		
Characteristic 3		
Characteristic 4		
Characteristic 5		

Venn Diagram

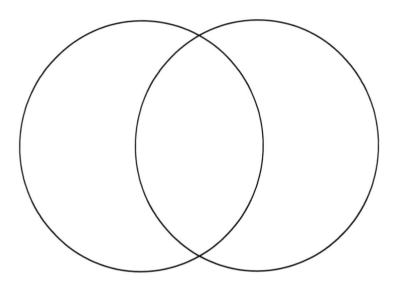

Sample Comparison and Contrast Essays

A Cell Phone Conversation and a Face-to-Face Conversation

Whether you have a conversation with someone on a cell phone or stand face to face and talk, it's all the same, right? It doesn't matter how you do it. Talking is about telling someone else what you think and listening to what the other person says. But is this all there is to talking? Consider what happens when you have a cell-phone conversation with someone versus how you communicate in a face-to-face conversation.

When you talk to someone on a cell phone, you're sharing all the information you can put into words. But you can't see the other person. You don't see the person's gestures or body language. You can't make eye-contact, which can tell you a lot about what the other person is thinking. She might be waving her arms in frustration or rolling her eyes, all the while keeping her voice calm and relaxed. She couldn't get away with that if she was standing in front of you. You'd see right off that all she wanted was to end the conversation.

On the other hand, whether you're on a cell phone or talking to someone in person, you both have to choose words to say what you mean. And in both cases, you can tell a lot about what the other person is thinking and feeling by listening to the person's tone.

So really, which is the best way to have a conversation, in person or on a cell phone? It seems like a simple answer. The face-to-face conversation gives you so much more information about what the person is thinking and feeling. Who'd want to use a cell phone if there was a choice between the two? Well, maybe someone who wanted to hide something. But of course, there is one legitimate time when a cell phone might be the best choice: when you're a long distance apart. Then, it's no contest.

Comparing and Contrasting Robots and People

Robots fascinate people, and for good reason: they can do a lot of the same things we humans do. But there are so many differences between humans and robots it's hard to think of them as being just like us.

To begin with, robots are machines. Many of them have arms and legs, or some kind of appendage, but they're made of steel and plastic and carbon fiber and wiring. As long as their batteries are well-charged they can work all day and all night and never get tired or sleepy. And their memories are vast and totally reliable. Like any computer, they can absorb a book in seconds and spit out quotes and facts and data on a moment's notice. And if their memory gets overloaded, someone can just stick in another hard drive. Robots, of course, don't have emotions, so you can't hurt their feelings, and they don't need other robots to keep them company. And finally, robots are not creative. They can think fast, but they can't think outside the box. Robots are just machines.

People, on the other hand, are organic, biological, human beings. They have muscle and fat and all kinds of soft tissue and liquids, but usually no plastic or carbon fiber or steel. People have pretty good memories, but we do forget lots of things and sometimes we get the facts wrong. Unlike robots, we do have emotions. We fall in love and get angry, and most of us will miss being around other people. Yes, people are kind of weak in a lot of ways compared to robots, but on the other hand, we can think outside the box. People are creative. Change our environment or stick an obstacle in our way, and we'll find a way around it or over it or through it.

Clearly, robots and humans are very different in many ways, but they are also a lot alike too. For example, both robots and people can think independently. We can both see and hear. Robots don't have eyes and ears exactly like humans do, but they have sensors that perform the same functions. By whatever name you call them, the sensors that humans and robots have enable them to monitor their environment, collect data about it, and then respond. For example, when someone sees something on the floor, such as a towel, he or she can pick it up. In the same way, a robot can be programmed to see a rock or anything else and pick it up. And both humans and robots can record data about this thing they've picked up. A robot might weigh the rock and determine its mineral content. A human might notice the towel is dirty and throw it in the laundry. And finally, both need fuel to operate. People get hungry and sit down and eat a meal. A robot starts running out of energy and plugs itself into the electrical outlet to charge up.

No one is going to mistake a robot for a person — at least not until robots get a lot more sophisticated. There are many things that are different about them, beginning with the fact that one is mechanical and the other is biological. On the other hand, humans and robots have a lot in common, more than you might think at first. They both can think independently, perceive their environment, and respond to it. And both need fuel to operate.

■ Crafting an Argument

For the Teacher

Defining the Strategy

Nearly all writing involves making an argument. In some way or another, every writer attempts to encourage readers to accept the ideas, characters, or images that the words represent. However, most analytical academic writing explicitly takes the form of argument, and this sort of writing emphasizes the use of claims based on merit and reasoning to convince an audience of a particular idea or issue. This is not narrative writing, which tells a story or relates historical events, and not informative writing, which is merely intended to explain or describe something. The chief characteristics of argument writing involve offering compelling reasons for the reader to accept the claim being made and also providing support to back up that claim. As a result of the conclusions presented by the writer, the reader may be expected to weigh the merits of the claim, change their thinking on the issue at hand, or take action. A strong written argument supports claims in an analysis of substantive topics or texts, using valid reasoning and relevant and sufficient evidence. The argument is expressed through clear and coherent writing in which the development, organization, and style are appropriate to the audience and purpose of the piece.

Crafting an argument begins in Quadrant B on the Rigor/Relevance Framework as writers apply their knowledge to justify a claim and then as they move through Quadrant C, analyzing and applying evidence to solve a problem. This process is completed in Quadrant D as students employ complex thinking to create solutions and take action within their conclusion to the argument.

Applying the Strategy

Argumentative writing is an effective strategy in most content areas and in middle and secondary programs.

Middle School

- Science
  - arguing the validity of the scientific method
  - offering proof of earth's origins
- Social Studies
  - drawing conclusions from primary resources
  - deducing the aspects of a civilization from its archeological record
  - arguing trends across centuries
- Math
  - solving word problems
  - interpreting graphs and charts
  - converting metric measurements
- ELA
  - argumentative essays
  - defining character and author point of view
  - book reviews

Secondary School

- Science
  - presenting biological theories
  - concluding proofs in physics
  - arguing for or against climate change

- Social Studies
  - arguing social theory
  - providing evidence of governmental function in civics
  - analyzing explanations of historical events
- Math
  - defining geometric proofs
  - arguing algebraic concepts
  - explaining functions and derivatives
- ELA
  - taking positions on literary theory
  - arguing for a particular poetic analysis
  - breaking down interpretations of novels and essays

Common Core State Standards

College and Career Readiness Anchor Standards for Writing

Text Types and Purposes

1. Write arguments to support claims in an analysis of substantive topics or texts, using valid reasoning and relevant and sufficient evidence.

2. Introduce precise, knowledgeable claim(s), establish the significance of the claim(s), distinguish the claim(s) from alternate or opposing claims, and create an organization that logically sequences claim(s), counterclaims, reasons, and evidence.

3. Develop claim(s) and counterclaims fairly and thoroughly, supplying the most relevant evidence for each while pointing out the strengths and limitations of both in a manner that anticipates the audience's knowledge level, concerns, values, and possible biases.

Production and Distribution of Writing

4. Produce clear and coherent writing in which the development, organization, and style are appropriate to task, purpose, and audience.

5. Develop and strengthen writing as needed by planning, revising, editing, rewriting, or trying a new approach.

Teaching the Strategy

Introduce the strategy by explaining that crafting an argument involves two major tasks for the writer:

- **Expressing a position.** An argument is a kind of monologue delivered from writer to reader. The writer challenges the reader to listen to a one-sided argument being presented. A good argument, though, is not just a series of complaints but a cleverly crafted or assembled set of ideas. These ideas can express an opinion on an issue or pose a solution to a problem. The writer's argument presents a singular point of view but by means of a thorough discussion; the points of view of others are considered and often shown to be false or contributing to the soundness of the writer's position. For example, a writer might express a position on campaign financing and in doing so advocate a solution that places a cap of $20 million on any given race.

- **Supporting that position.** When crafting an argument, it's not enough for the writer to merely state an opinion or list random ideas. Support for that opinion both validates the writer's ideas and seeks to persuade readers with evidence that is irrefutable. A solid argument is built on facts and assumptions that lead to a logical conclusion. The writer of the argument brings the reader along with his or her thinking by appealing to reason. Solid support also anticipates and answers any objections that a critic of the writer's position may advance. For example, one of the supporting details for a crafted argument might be the results of a public opinion poll showing that the vast majority of high school students would prefer that school start later in the morning.

Writing a well-crafted argument requires a method of organization that presents the writer's claim or position, any supporting reasoning, any evidence and details, as well as any counterclaims and summaries or conclusions. The format chosen can vary, but a well-organized presentation will help readers follow the writer's thread of logic and interlinked reasoning.

Any graphic organizer presenting the structure of the writer's argument will vary with the elements used; nevertheless, this basic layout will demonstrate the flow of thinking and the path the reader will have to follow to be successfully persuaded by an instance of analytical argument writing. Look over this sample graphic organizer and note the order of presentation.

Elements of Argument

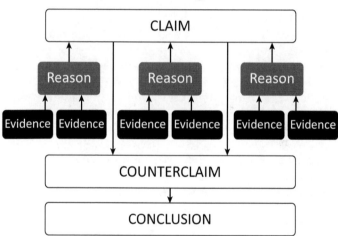

A written argument begins with the writer staking a **claim** or taking a **position**. This can be an **assertion** of his or her **point of view** on a topic. Point of view in argument is not the same as a point of view in fiction, which describes the viewpoint or perspective of a character. The author of an argument is asserting an opinion in an argument that is restated in a variety of ways:

- **Theme.** When writers try to prove a claim, they often develop a larger theme, as is done in a novel or an essay. This theme is a controlling set of ideas that presents the fully fleshed-out intention of an author. A theme is a broader answer than a simple claim of fact.

- **Proposition.** The author's argument is often an assertion that is proposed as a solution and then proven to be useful or true.

- **Main idea and purpose.** An argument has a main or controlling idea, similar to the sentences in a paragraph or article that summarize the overall concept of the work. The author's main idea should help the reader understand whatever central purpose prompted the piece of writing in the first place.

Support for a position can take a variety of forms, typically **reasons, evidence,** and **details.** Reasons are statements that declare ideas in support of an argument. There may be primary, secondary, or other ranked reasons, based on their importance. Reasons are often linked to specific evidence. If you are arguing for a raise, you may state as a reason that your efforts increased company's profits. Evidence, in this case, might be a chart of facts, illustrating how what you did resulted in specific higher sales. Evidence can also come in the form of quotations, examples, or qualified opinions that support your claim. Of course, evidence can and should be taken from multiple print and digital sources, and should be attributed appropriately to avoid plagiarism. Your evidence, in the end, should support your analysis, reflection, and research.

A **counterargument** is a necessary admission by the writer that other viewpoints may exist. Strong arguments introduce opposing positions and then demonstrate why they are false or weak and how they fail to counter the argument being made.

- **Other Points of View.** Reasonable readers want to consider other critical opinions and contrary facts than those that come from the writer's point of view. After they have been given the chance to compare alternative points of view, readers will feel more comfortable embracing the argument being presented.

- **Assumptions.** On any side of an argument, certain opinions or beliefs are taken for granted. These basic assumptions often form the foundation of the argument. Writers of measured arguments use these fundamental assumptions to strengthen their position and convince doubters that their claim is an accepted principle. If readers share assumptions with the writer, they are likely to be convinced. If readers don't share a writer's assumptions, the writer may have to make those assumptions explicit and defend them.

The **conclusion** can be a simple restatement of the claim or thesis. It can also contain a **recommendation** for action to be taken as a result of the argument. In addition, it can advance **other related arguments** or **summaries**.

Directed Writing Activity

1. This activity will require students to produce clear and coherent writing in which development, organization, and style are appropriate to task and purpose. Select a topic about which any reader would have an opinion. This can be a school-related issue or a concern of the average student of their age and background. Students should have prior knowledge of the topic so they can craft an argument without needing to conduct additional research. For example, they might argue that students should be able to choose the amount of homework they feel is adequate to learn the material. This is a topic any student could argue for or against.

2. As appropriate to your class and the topic, copy and distribute the argument diagram form, or allow them to modify or create one that suits their purposes. Both a blank diagram form and a completed one are provided.

3. Ask students to think carefully about the topic, first just listing basic claims and reasons on their graphic organizers.

4. Develop a class organizer with students' help. Have students guide you in labeling it correctly.

5. Discuss the claim being crafted in the argument. Invite students to share ideas from their own organizers, and add these points to the class organizer. Add additional boxes as necessary to accommodate various responses.

6. Discuss reasons and evidence, and enter ideas in the appropriate portion of the organizer.

Sample Organizer

Homework Argument

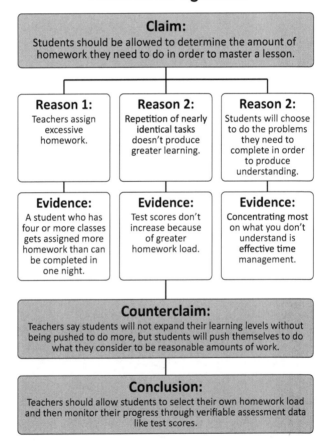

Claim:
Students should be allowed to determine the amount of homework they need to do in order to master a lesson.

Reason 1:
Teachers assign excessive homework.

Reason 2:
Repetition of nearly identical tasks doesn't produce greater learning.

Reason 2:
Students will choose to do the problems they need to complete in order to produce understanding.

Evidence:
A student who has four or more classes gets assigned more homework than can be completed in one night.

Evidence:
Test scores don't increase because of greater homework load.

Evidence:
Concentrating most on what you don't understand is effective time management.

Counterclaim:
Teachers say students will not expand their learning levels without being pushed to do more, but students will push themselves to do what they consider to be reasonable amounts of work.

Conclusion:
Teachers should allow students to select their own homework load and then monitor their progress through verifiable assessment data like test scores.

7. Discuss possible counterclaims and conclusions. Point out how the evidence presented should anticipate any counterclaims. Review, as necessary, the components of an essay, including the introduction and lively writing free of cliché. Then instruct students to write a six- or seven-paragraph essay crafting their particular argument on the issue, using the format shown in the chart on the preceding page. Remind them that they can use points discussed in the whole class example as well. Urge them to consider the development, organization, and style of their writing as well as its purpose. They can also incorporate research if they wish.

8. After learners complete their essays, review and discuss the assignment. Encourage students to describe the organizers they used and why they chose them. Ask students how they organized their essays and to explain their choices. Invite students to consider what they would do differently if given this assignment again.

9. Assign the independent writing activity.

Reference

Jones, R. *Rigor and Relevance Handbook*. Rexford, NY: International Center for Leadership in Education, 2010.

For the Student

Independent Writing Activity

Follow these directions to write a crafted argument essay. Develop your writing appropriately by planning, revising, and editing. You may also research details as necessary.

1. Choose a controversial topic that you know well and write a complete argument essay. Here are some topic suggestions:

   - banning the use of cell phones in public enclosed places like trains or buses

   - the ethics of de-friending someone on social media sites

   - the need to provide alternative foods at a party for those who restrict their diets

   - the phenomenon of people who talk back to the movie in a theater

   - people spending billions on pet food while millions of people starve

2. Identify your claim or position on these issues or decide on one of your own. Select a type of argument from the following table.

Types of Argument

Authority	Logic	Deductive/Inductive
The writer is an expert or has prior knowledge.	Logical relationship between claim and support.	Start with a general claim, then facts, then close with a specific or sweeping conclusion.
Evidence can include insider knowledge, quotes, qualified opinions, provable observations.	Cause and effect is an example. The evidence presented follows a rational order of thinking.	Facts and evidence lead to an unavoidable conclusion. Inductive reasoning requires a probable conclusion.
Strength: experience	*Strength*: common sense	*Strength*: its basis in facts
Weakness: credibility	*Weakness*: opinion	*Weakness*: a false premise leads to a false conclusion or overgeneralization

3. Complete a graphic organizer that organizes your argument. Adapt its form as necessary.

4. Choose a method of organizing your essay. Select a type of claim from the following table.

Types of Claims

Fact (Substantiation)	Value (Evaluation)	Policy (Recommendation)
Claim that something exists or that it is a fact	Claim about the value of something	Claim that something should be done
Example: *Standardized test scores have improved over the last ten years.*	Example: *Standardized tests are an effective way to measure student achievement.*	Example: *We should replace standardized tests with portfolio assessment.*

5. Write a six- or seven-paragraph argument about your topic. Remember to include an introduction and a conclusion. Conduct research if necessary.

6. Use the Argument Writing Rubric that follows to self-grade your argument. Share yours with a classmate and see if they agree with your scoring on the rubric.

Argument Graphic Organizer

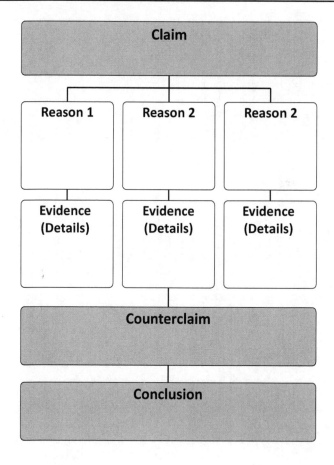

Argument Writing Rubric

Criteria	Insufficient 1	Developing 2	Sufficient 3	Exemplary 4	Score
The introduction clearly states the writer's claim, or thesis statement	Needs a thesis statement that states the writer's claim	Includes the writer's claim, but it is unclear	Thesis statement clearly states the writer's claim	Compelling thesis statement clearly states the writer's claim	
Strong reasons and evidence support the writer's claim.	Needs supporting reasons and evidence	Includes reason(s) or evidence that are not convincing or relevant	Includes at least two convincing reasons and textual evidence	Includes three or more convincing reasons and textual evidence	
The writer includes a counterclaim and response.	Needs a counterclaim and response	Includes one counterclaim, but there is no response, or the response is unrelated	Includes at least one counterclaim and response with strong evidence	Includes two counterclaims and responses with strong evidence	
The writer includes citation information for textual evidence.	No textual evidence or citation information	One or two pieces of textual evidence with incorrect citation information	Two or more pieces of textual evidence with correct citation information	Various textual evidence (paraphrased/ quoted) with correct citation information	

Criteria	Insufficient 1	Developing 2	Sufficient 3	Exemplary 4	Score
Transitions introduce reasons and evidence.	Needs transition words or phrases	One or two transition words or phrases that introduce reasons and evidence	Three or more transition words or phrases that introduce reasons and evidence	Variety of transition words or phrases effectively introduce reasons and evidence	
The conclusion restates a thesis and offers a recommendation.	Needs a recommendation or recommendation is off-topic.	Offers a recommendation but it is not meaningful or actionable	Offers a recommendation related to the thesis	Offers a meaningful and actionable recommendation	
The writing follows conventions of mechanics, spelling, and usage.	Errors in grammar, spelling, punctuation, and capitalization that impede reader understanding	Some errors in grammar, spelling, punctuation, and capitalization	Few errors in grammar, spelling, punctuation, and capitalization	Correct grammar, spelling, punctuation, and capitalization	
				Overall Score	

Crafting a Research Statement

Defining the Strategy

You or your students may remember the days when writing a research paper simply meant locating facts about a topic and rephrasing them into a paper. Today's world requires much more. Today's 21st-century learners need to develop ideas and opinions grounded in fact and logic. They also need to draw evidence from literary or informational texts to support analysis, reflection, and research. To draw conclusions and form claims, students charged with these tasks must organize and analyze the content of their research. Then, their conclusions and claims must be concisely stated in one or more sentences known as the research statement (or thesis). After students have collected evidence and categorized their information based on certain criteria, they are then ready to craft a research statement.

The main objective of crafting a research statement is to draw conclusions and synthesize information. Crafting such a statement requires a student to analyze and evaluate ideas as well as construct opinions or claims based on research. These processes add rigor and relevance to a student's learning as he or she uses information in a new way that is appropriate to task, purpose, and audience. These practices solidly place this strategy within Quadrant D on the Rigor/Relevance Framework.

Applying the Strategy

Teaching students to craft a research statement is an effective strategy in most content areas in middle and secondary programs.

Middle School

- Science
    - researching volcanoes to determine how their presence affects the environment and our lives
- Social Studies
    - researching recent inventions to determine which have had the most impact on a student's school day
- Math
    - researching a famous mathematician to determine how his or her work has changed society
- ELA
    - researching words added to dictionaries over the last few years and reflecting on what these changes tell us about our society

Secondary School

- Science
    - researching advances in genetic mapping to determine what applications this technology should have, if any, in our daily lives
- Social Studies
    - researching the impact of large chain stores, such as Wal-Mart, on a community to determine whether their presence helps or hurts the community

- Math
    - researching how to determine the most efficient route when configuring delivery routes, ambulance routes, or garbage collection routes and applying this information to a route used in your city
- ELA
    - researching and analyzing the works of a famous poet to determine the poet's style

Common Core State Standards

College and Career Readiness Anchor Standards for Writing

Production and Distribution of Writing

4. Produce clear and coherent writing in which the development, organization, and style are appropriate to task, purpose, and audience.

Research to Build and Present Knowledge

7. Conduct short as well as more sustained research projects based on focused questions, demonstrating understanding of the subject under investigation.

9. Draw evidence from literary or informational text to support analysis, reflection, and research.

Teaching the Strategy

Explain that writing a research statement is one task during the middle of the writing process, often at the beginning of the writing stage. Before writing a research statement, students will most likely have done the following:

- Chosen or identified the research topic
- Conducted initial research on the topic
- Developed research questions as necessary to investigate the topic further
- Set the purpose for writing (e.g., to inform, to give an opinion, to persuade) and determined the audience
- Organized and analyzed information

Emphasize that presenting research is more than just retelling information from various sources. You conduct research to answer a question or develop an opinion. This answer to your question or your opinion, as the case may be, is the focus of your results and is often called the research statement, or thesis. To more efficiently create a research statement, be sure to clarify a topic, question, and its significance early in the research process.

Also remember that a research product may not be a paper; you may create a research statement for a speech or PowerPoint presentation. Completing the following statements may help you identify your research topic, purpose, and/or audience:

- I am conducting research on _____ for an audience that includes _____.
- I hope to learn _____ because _____.
- In this (product) _____, my goal is to _____ my audience (about/that) _____.

You can use your statements to develop your main research question. Examples:

- I am conducting research on tornados for an audience that includes students and teachers who have experienced the threat of tornados.

- I hope to learn about recent developments in early warning detection because I want people to be better prepared for tornadoes.

- In this paper, my goal is to inform my audience about how technology can help protect people from tornadoes.

From these statements, you can focus your attention on one specific question about tornados: How can we use modern technology to better protect people from tornadoes? The succinct answer to this question is your research statement: Developing technology such as the CASA radar system and commercial airplane weather sensors may allow communities to better forecast and detect tornadoes.

You may also consider the answers to the following questions to help develop your research statement:

- What have you read about _____?
- What opinions can you form about _____?
- What evidence can you use to support your opinion that _____?
- What do you need to explore further about _____?

Once you have your purpose, audience, and focus in mind, you can write your research statement. An effective research statement has the following qualities:

- Makes a concise statement about your topic
- Makes a specific and significant statement about your topic
- Implies your purpose
- Considers the audience
- Suggests the scope or organization of your statement

Examples:

- Fad diets can be dangerous when you do not supply the body with essential nutrients or when you depend on excessive quantities of potentially harmful foods.

In this example, the concise, specific, and significant statement is the danger of fad diets. Notice that the author presents an opinion or conclusion, not a fact, about the topic. The scope or organization of the argument involves what happens when you lack nutrients and ingest excessive quantities of harmful foods. The reader can expect the author to elaborate on these two areas within the paper to prove his or her point. The implied purpose is to give an opinion and inform.

- Using therapeutic communication can improve patient outcomes by encouraging positive interaction, promoting openness, and supporting personal accountability.

   In this example, the concise, specific, and significant statement is the positive impact of using therapeutic communication with patients. Notice that the author does not try to tackle everything involved with therapeutic communication; he or she focuses on how therapeutic communication improves patient outcomes. The scope or organization of the statement is positive interaction, openness, and personal accountability. The implied purpose is to inform.

The research statement may be an argument or claim supported by reasons and evidence. An argument may be one of the following:

- **Substantiation:** claim of fact that tries to prove the existence or truthfulness of something

   Example: Global warming is not the cause of changing weather patterns.

- **Evaluation:** claim of value that argues that one thing is better or worse than another

   Example: Tornados are the most destructive storms.

- **Recommendation:** claim of policy that calls for a specific action

   Example: We should build permanent storm shelters in our community.

Directed Writing Activity

1. This activity will require students to conduct a short research project based on focused questions and demonstrate an understanding of the subject. Students will draw evidence from informational texts to support analysis and reflection and will ultimately develop a research statement. Explain to students that the school board has begun to investigate the role of vending machines in the school. They are asking students to attend the next school board meeting to express their opinions on the topic. Introduce students to each of the following digital sources about foods in schools.

    http://www.fns.usda.gov/tn/resources/m_app5.pdf

    http://www.nytimes.com/2011/10/04/education/04vending.html?_r=1&pagewanted=all

    http://www.cdc.gov/healthyyouth/nutrition/pdf/nutrition_factsheet_parents.pdf

2. After students have read through the sources, ask them to identify more specific topics (e.g., effects of vending machines on student health). Generate questions with students about the topics. Examples may include the following:

    *   Are there benefits of having vending machines in schools?
    *   How have vending machines negatively impacted student health?
    *   Should schools completely eliminate vending machines?
    *   How can schools keep vending machines while also improving student health?

3. Encourage students to choose a question that interests them and, if necessary, complete additional research to answer the question.

4. Work with students to identify the topic, audience, and purpose for their research statement.

5. If students struggle, encourage them to use the statements and questions in "Teaching the Strategy" to identify a focus for their research statement.

6. Finally, ask students to develop a research statement based on their initial research and analysis.

7. Ask students to share their research statements with the class. Allow students to evaluate the research statements based on the qualities listed in Teaching the Strategy.

8. Assign the independent writing activity.

Reference

InTASC Model Core Teaching Standards: A Resource for State Dialogue.

For the Student

Independent Writing Activity

1. Follow these directions to conduct a short research project in order to draw evidence from informational texts and develop a research statement.

2. Much of the news about schools these days involves budget cuts that school corporations have been forced to make. Your school is facing budget cuts and has considered cuts in art, music, athletic programs, busing programs, after-school clubs, and the number of school days in the year. Students have been asked to present their reasoning for why certain cuts should or should not be made in the form of a letter to the superintendent.

3. Conduct initial research about the benefits of some of the programs or the consequences that may result from cutting certain programs or shortening the school year.

4. Use the "Crafting a Research Statement" document to generate questions, focus the topic of your letter, and develop your research statement.

5. Evaluate your research statement based on the following criteria:
   - Does it make a concise statement about your topic?
   - Does it make a specific and significant statement about your topic?
   - Does it imply your purpose?
   - Does it consider your audience?
   - Does it suggest the scope or organization of your research project?

6. Revise your research statement based on your evaluation. Write your revised research statement below.

_____

_____

Crafting a Research Statement

Use this guide to develop questions and a research statement to provide focus for your research.

1. **General topic:** In one to three words, what is your topic about?

   _____

2. **Begin research:** Start skimming through the resources available on this topic. As you read, pay attention to what captures your interest or causes you to ask questions.

3. **Audience:** Ask yourself, "Who do I want to read my research? Who would be interested in it?"

   _____

4. **Purpose:** Ask yourself, "What is the purpose of presenting my research (e.g., entertain, inform, give an opinion, persuade)?"

5. **Ask questions:** What questions does your initial reading make you wonder about?

   _____

   _____

   _____

6. **Focus and hypothesize:** Highlight a question that narrows your topic and captures your interest. Then reframe the question as a statement that answers the question and expresses your view.

   _____

   _____

7. **Scope and organization:** How you do intend to defend or organize your claim? Add the scope to your research statement by adding to your statement in #5 or by adding a second sentence.

   _____

   _____

Evaluating a Digital Source

For the Teacher

Defining the Strategy

With a vast sea of information available through the Internet and other digital sources, the question today's students face is not whether information exists on a subject but whether the information is credible and accurate. During the prewriting stage, students are often tasked with gathering relevant information from sources, assessing the credibility and accuracy of each source, and determining how that information affects the ideas that will ultimately make up their writing. In order to incorporate digital sources successfully, students need the skills to evaluate a website for the integrity of its information and author. In order to develop these students into effective 21st-century learners, we must not only teach and model these skills but also impress upon them the importance of such evaluation.

The main objective of evaluating a digital source is to draw conclusions about, and appraise the value of, the information it provides. These processes add rigor and relevance to the learning of students because they must make judgments about what is stated or inferred in a text. Creating a more competent and confident learner in the classroom and beyond, this strategy solidly fits within Quadrant D on the Rigor/Relevance Framework.

Applying the Strategy

Teaching students to evaluate a digital source is an effective strategy in all content areas and in middle and secondary programs.

Middle School

- Science
  - locating three reliable digital sources to start your own garden
- Social Studies
  - finding three credible digital sources to create a tourist pamphlet about historical sites in your city, county, or state
- Math
  - researching the cost of natural disasters in the United States within the last five years to create a graph displaying the information
- ELA
  - using biographies of an author to determine how the events in the author's life or time period affected a piece of literature

Secondary School

- Science
  - finding two conflicting digital sources about the topic of global warming and evaluate their conclusions
- Social Studies
  - using the Internet to compare and contrast a primary and secondary source about the same event or time period (e.g., battle in World War II, the Civil War period)

- Math
  - researching to find three credible resources on the Internet for students who are interested in pursuing a career in engineering
- ELA
  - using the Internet to find two reviews of a work of literature, evaluating how each interprets the text

Common Core State Standards

College and Career Readiness Anchor Standards for Writing

Research to Build and Present Knowledge

7. Conduct short as well as more sustained research projects based on focused questions, demonstrating understanding of the subject under investigation.

8. Gather relevant information from multiple print and digital sources, assess the credibility and accuracy of each source, and integrate the information while avoiding plagiarism.

Teaching the Strategy

Introduce the evaluation of digital sources by explaining how easy it is for anyone to post information on the Internet. People of all ages and backgrounds can publish information on a website or electrical document. They only need a computer and access to the Internet. In this kind of information environment, evaluating the sources you find online is essential to becoming an effective researcher.

How Do I Find Credible Sources?

The search for finding credible sources begins with an effective online search. Begin by brainstorming words associated with the topic. In order to do this, you may need to preview some sources on your topic. For example, if you are researching global warming, you may read an online encyclopedia article about it and then come up with key words such as *weather, environment, North Pole, ozone,* and *carbon dioxide.*

You will likely pull up many sources on the topic. Refine your search choices by building phrases from your key words. For example, "ozone in the North Pole" will narrow your search and help you find specific credible sources more quickly.

Using different search engines and sites to search may also help you find more credible sources. Popular search engines include Google, Yahoo, and Lycos; however, you can also use specific directories and databases to find high-quality information. Some examples include Librarian's Index, Finding Dulcinea, Findarticle.com, American Memory, Mayo Clinic, CIA World Fact Book, and many others.

Who Is the Author and/or Publisher of the Source?

Explain that one way to identify a reliable source is to look at the author or sponsor of the site. Consider the following when identifying the author:

- What is the author's educational background or credentials?
- What has the author published?
- What is the author's experience in the field?
- What institution or organization is the author affiliated with?

The website may not identify an author; however, you may be able to determine which organization or institution sponsors the site. Looking at the URL address is one way to do this. For example in the address http://www.si.edu/ResearchCenters, the first part of the URL address (SI) tells who publishes the article (Smithsonian), and the second part (edu) tells additional information about the kind of site. In this case it is an educational site. Other common sites include the following:

- .gov = government website
- .org = not-for-profit organization website
- .com = commercial or business website
- .net = network infrastructures
- .mil = U.S. military branch

Anything after the backslash following the second part of the address also gives information about the topic or form of the website. In this case, the URL address directs you to the research part of the website. This information can help you determine the reliability of a site. For example, a for-profit business website that may be trying to sell something may not be as reliable as a website dedicated to education.

What Is the Purpose of the Source?

Tell students that a second way to evaluate a digital source is by considering a source's purpose. The Internet has many different kinds of sites in which you may find information.

- personal home pages maintained by individuals
- special interest sites maintained by non-profit organizations or activists dealing with special issues
- professional sites maintained by institutions or organizations
- news and journalistic sites maintained by national news agencies, international news agencies, online newspapers, and magazine publications
- commercial sites maintained by businesses

Determine whether the purpose of a source is to persuade (or call someone to action) or to inform. Some sources may involve a combination of both. For example, a special interest site may give information about a topic but then ask the reader to do something. Carefully evaluate these sources and consider why a source presents information. Then determine whether the purpose of the source meets your needs for research. Generally, you will want a source just dedicated to informing others.

What Are the Characteristics of the Content?

Explain that evaluating a source also involves analyzing the content of the site.

- Does the source relate to your topic? Does the source just contain general information, or does it give specific facts related to your topic?
- Is the information well researched? Is it supported by credible references?
- Is the information accurate?
- Is the information factual or does it contain opinions?
- Is the information only a summary or abstract from a more complete source?
- Is the source current? When was the site last updated?
- Does the website link to other reliable sites?
- Is the site or web document professional? Are there errors in spelling, grammar, or punctuation?

Answering these questions can help you determine whether a site is reliable and useful for your research.

Directed Research Activity

1. This activity will require students to assess the credibility and accuracy of digital sources in order to gather relevant, credible information. Introduce students to each of the following digital sources about changes in the adolescent brain.

- Source 1: http://www.pbs.org/wgbh/pages/frontline/shows/teenbrain/work/adolescent.html
- Source 2: http://www.thenationalcampaign.org/resources/pdf/BRAIN.pdf
- Source 3: http://www.nimh.nih.gov/health/publications/the-teen-brain-still-under-construction/complete-index.shtml
- Source 4: http://www.aea267.k12.ia.us/r4/index.php?page=r4-adolescent-brain
- Source 5: http://www.naiku.net/blog/teenage-mind-and-naiku/

Discuss with students key words and phrases that may have helped find these sources. Sample: *adolescent brain, cognitive changes, adolescent development, adolescent behavior.*

2. Introduce students to the Evaluating Digital Sources worksheet by filling out the form for source 1 with students. Ensure students understand what to fill in for Title ("Adolescent Brains Are Works in Progress") Source/Website URL (www.pbs.org), and Publisher (Frontline producer Sarah Spinks). Answer any questions students may have as you move through the worksheet evaluating the source.

3. Once you have completed the worksheet for source 1, ask students to pair up and fill out the worksheet for one of the remaining sources. Ensure that all sources are being evaluated by at least one pair of students. Rotate around the room and answer questions as they arise.

4. After students have finished filling out the worksheet for one of the sources, come together as a class to discuss the remaining four sources. Ask questions and challenge students as appropriate to help them sharpen their evaluative skills.

5. Finally, have students rank each of the five sources in terms of credibility and accuracy. Discuss students' rankings as a class. Ask students to determine which sources would be appropriate to include in a research report about changes in the adolescent brain and which ones should not be used.

6. Ask students about their perceived ability to evaluate the credibility and accuracy of a digital source. Remind students about the ways they can evaluate a source (considering author/publisher, considering purpose, and considering content) and the tools they can use (Evaluating Digital Sources worksheet). Have students reflect on the importance of such evaluation.

7. Assign the independent research activity.

Reference

InTASC Model Core Teaching Standards: A Resource for State Dialogue.

For the Student

Independent Research Activity

Follow these directions to conduct research about how technology has affected parenting. Use advanced searches effectively to find digital sources that are credible, accurate, and appropriate for the topic.

1. Determine key words and phrases that would be appropriate for a search. Create a word web if necessary.

    _____   _____   _____

2. List three search engines and/or directories that would be appropriate to use for your search.

    _____

    _____

    _____

3. Conduct your search. Refine your search as necessary to find digital sources appropriate for your topic. After briefly reviewing your search results, choose three digital sources that seem credible, accurate, and appropriate.

4. Use the Evaluating Digital Sources worksheet to evaluate your three sources. Fill out a form for each of your sources.

5. After evaluating your sources, rank them based on credibility, accuracy, and appropriateness. Provide a brief explanation of your ranking.

    *   Source 1: _____

        _____

        _____

    *   Source 2: _____

        _____

        _____

- Source 3: _____

  _____

  _____

6. How would you rate your search (expert, proficient, novice, beginner)? Explain.

   _____

   _____

7. How confident do you feel in your ability to evaluate digital sources based on credibility, accuracy, and usefulness (very confident, somewhat confident, not confident)? Explain.

   _____

   _____

Evaluating Digital Sources

Title: Source/Website URL: Publisher:		
Author/Publisher	**Yes**	**No**
Does the author have credentials and/or experience directly related to the topic?		
Is the publisher reliable?		
Purpose		
Is the main purpose of the source to inform?		
Does the purpose of the source meet my needs?		
Content		
Does the source relate to my topic?		
Does the source contain too much general information?		
Does the source contain specific facts related to my topic?		
Is the information well researched?		
Is the information merely a summary or abstract of a more complete source?		
Is the source current, or has it recently been updated?		
For websites: Does the website link to other reliable sites?		
Are there errors in spelling, grammar, or punctuation?		
How would you rate this source? Circle your answer. Excellent Good Fair Poor		
This source is not useful for _____ _____ _____ _____		

Integrating Visual Evidence

For the Teacher

Defining the Strategy

The heart and soul of any analytical academic writing is the research a writer has conducted prior to producing the paper itself. But solid research goes beyond successful manipulation of online search engines or library and database card catalogues. Even when students successfully acquire lots of valuable information from a wide variety of valuable sources, they often fail to use a potentially quite powerful tool: visual evidence. Many types of visual evidence are easy to locate today: images, photographs, charts, organizers, illustrations, artwork, videos, and multimedia sources like PowerPoint presentations or podcasts. While these types of evidence may not, to some, seem ideal for the traditional 8½ x 11-inch paper research paper, students who manage to integrate these forms of visual evidence actually bring an increased level of sophistication to their work and can heighten the impact of their proofs and reasoning as a result. For a readership that is increasingly being raised on the Internet, simple sentences may not be as moving or even illustrative as a slide show, embedded video, or interactive data presentation.

Common Core State Standards clearly acknowledge the changing media landscape's impact on writing, research, and audience expectations. The CCSS, in fact, cite varied media as an example of the sort of complex information that should be included whether they are writing informative or explanatory texts. Moreover, the CCSS encourage students to examine and convey complex ideas, concepts, and information clearly and accurately through the effective selection, organization, and analysis of various sorts of visually focused content, including formatting (e.g., headings), graphics (e.g., figures, tables), and multimedia when these factors aid comprehension. The strategy of integrating visual evidence works well, in particular, with the Paraphrasing Writing Strategy and Scaffolding Note-taking, especially when students are developing research papers or projects.

The Rigor/Relevance Framework, as well as the CCSS, calls for students to embrace technological applications and apply them to their processes of learning. A variety of visual and audio sources that include graphics, charges, images, and so on are — more and more — enhancing student learning, In fact, multimedia software is changing education more broadly by providing a wellspring of fresh approaches and information sources. With the proliferation of this software, it is increasingly easy for students to take advantage of these applications. In the *Rigor and Relevance Handbook,* Richard Jones states, "The students of tomorrow will be communicating ideas in visual form with audio background because it is so easy to edit multimedia material . . . . Technology puts vast amounts of knowledge at students' fingertips . . . . Technology offers students a chance to delve deeply into a topic." The chart **Technology Applications for Rigorous and Relevant Learning** in this section lists a few ways that students can use technology for learning in each quadrant.

Applying the Strategy

Integrating visual evidence is an effective strategy in most content areas and in middle and secondary programs.

Middle School

- Science
  - biome population illustrations
  - videos demonstrating the laws of physics
  - graphs of earth science data
  - timelines of geologic eras

- Social Studies
  - political cartoons
  - lithographs
  - painted portraits or busts of historical figures
  - architectural layouts of ruins and early civilizations
  - photos of current events
- Math
  - 3D representations of geometric figures
  - demonstrations of word problem data
  - graphs of data
  - puzzles and charts
- ELA
  - graphic representations and outlines of plots
  - illustrations of books
  - photos of authors

Secondary School

- Science
  - anatomical diagrams
  - models of atomic structures
  - the periodic table of elements
  - time-lapse videos of scientific processes
  - simulations of invisible events
- Social Studies
  - hyperlinks of ongoing research projects
  - newspaper photographs and etchings
  - geophysical satellite representations

- Math
  - sine/cosine and parabola graphs and other trigonometry functions
  - geometric drawings
  - wave behavior and optics graphics
- ELA
  - dramatic stagings
  - historical records of fictionalized events
  - recordings of poets and writers
  - background music for movies

Common Core State Standards

College and Career Readiness Anchor Standards for Writing

Text Types and Purposes

1. Write arguments to support claims in an analysis of substantive topics or texts, using valid reasoning and relevant and sufficient evidence.

2. Write informative/explanatory texts to examine and convey complex ideas and information clearly and accurately through the effective selection, organization, and analysis of content.

3. Write narratives to develop real or imagined experiences or events using effective technique, well-chosen details, and well-structured event sequences.

Production and Distribution of Writing

4. Produce clear and coherent writing in which the development, organization, and style are appropriate to task, purpose, and audience.

5. Develop and strengthen writing as needed by planning, revising, editing, rewriting, or trying a new approach.

6. Use technology, including the Internet, to produce and publish writing and to interact and collaborate with others.

Research to Build and Present Knowledge

7. Conduct short as well as more sustained research projects based on focused questions, demonstrating understanding of the subject under investigation.

8. Gather relevant information from multiple print and digital sources, assess the credibility and accuracy of each source, and integrate the information while avoiding plagiarism.

Teaching the Strategy

Introduce the strategy by explaining that a wide variety of visual evidence is available to be incorporated in any report. How students choose to include it depends on both the topic they are analyzing and the format they have chosen. Some of the visual elements to consider are:

- **Print Photos:** Students can copy photos from books, magazines, or other print sources. To be used in an electronic form, photos can be converted to jpg or pdf files after a copy or the original printed photo is scanned and uploaded. Proper credit should always be given.

- **Online Photos:** These photos can be located within the research itself, particularly on websites with illustrations. Students can select and copy them or drop and drag them into a new document, giving proper credit, of course. Other photo sources can also be accessed using search engines, which usually offer the option of displaying images when a student enters the topic or the search command. Some search engines require that the student specify "images of. . . ." Students can scroll through archives of the related images located via search engines, but should always click on the image and visit the site it came from, since often the image may not be related to the topic searched, or may be improperly identified by the search criteria.

- ○ **Flicker, Photobucket, and other photo-sharing sites:** There may be restrictions on the use of the photos that are posted by users to these sites, but many photographers allow private individuals to use their images. To see any downloading restrictions, right-click on a PC or hold down the Control Key on a Mac and click on the photo. Photo-sharing sites can be searched by topic or group. While this kind of search will require students to look through archived photos, it can also help them decide which images they want and also introduce them to visuals they may not have considered. Social media sites also provide photo sharing.

- ○ **Stock footage:** Like stock photo sources, these sites can also provide video clips suitable to any platform, and these clips can be mixed with still photos and audio as well.

- ○ **Encyclopedias and/or databases:** There may be a fee involved for accessing the full service connections of encyclopedia sites that allow students to locate photos, video, political cartoons, illustrations, and primary source documents on particular topics.

- **Video Clips:** Students can locate video sources with a search engine in much the same manner as they search images. These clips will be displayed in archives like photos and have to be screened and reviewed for their appropriateness. A wide variety of sites offer informational videos, like Educational Videos.com, Watch-KnowLearn.com, or RefSeek, which itself provides links to many other educational sites. Another useful resource is Discovery Education Streaming, a pay service like Encyclopedia Britannica or World Book online. In short, there are plenty of choices beyond YouTube or Metacafe.

- **Multimedia:** The most common presentation of this sort is the PowerPoint slide show. PowerPoint presentations are easy to display and easy to construct from photos, audio, and text sources. They also allow for a wide variety of ways to organize and present graphics. Topic searches may return already completed Power-

Point presentations. Look for the .ppt extension and logo on hits for your topic.

○ **Slide shows, movie makers:** Almost every computer today comes with the software for converting photographs, music, audio narration, or movies into slide shows or video. These can be burned to disc or posted online for viewers to access. Various websites will also provide this service with professional effects like pan or zoom transitions.

○ **Reviews of electronic resources:** A number of universities and libraries offer reviews of websites and other web sources that evaluate the visual elements and accuracy of those sites.

○ **Video collections:** Many searches for popular topics will often yield a variety of image sources, including hypercard stacks, interactive modules, and special software. One such site allows viewers to explore archeological dig sites in South America from the comfort of their home, switching back and forth between different visuals.

Locating visual resources is the first step, but before students can apply what they have found they must first conduct a careful review. The Directed Writing Activity will help them analyze the resources they have found. After multiple viewings, students will be able to isolate information and visuals that could be useful to their written academic writing. They will then decide how to integrate these materials in their report.

Consult this chart for different ways you can help guide students when they are using visual technologies resources to prepare an analytical academic paper. In the *Rigor and Relevance Handbook,* Richard Jones illustrates where various technology applications fit into the Rigor/Relevance Framework.

Technology Applications for Rigorous and Relevant Learning

Quadrant C Assimilation	Quadrant D Adaptation
• Use word processing for writing and editing reports. • Use spreadsheets for analyzing research data. • Use presentation software for presentations. • Use Internet sources for research. • Create graphic organizers to record ideas.	• Develop multimedia presentations. • Do project design. • Research potential solutions to problems. • Prepare mock-ups of designs. • Present information in the form of WebQuests.
Quadrant A Acquisition	Quadrant B Application
• Do drill and practice for basic skills. • Take online quizzes for review. • Take notes on computers and hand-held devices. • Develop basic writing through word processing. • Create graphic organizers to record ideas.	• View demonstrations online. • Collaborate with other students via the Internet. • Collect data in the field with hand-held devices. • Use spreadsheets for analyzing collected data. • Learn procedures through computer simulations. • Use business software applications. • Research careers online.

Directed Writing Activity

Go over the recording document that follows to demonstrate how students should use this tool during their multiple viewings of the visual resources they have researched.

1. **Viewing Notes Chart.** Students should have a pen ready and a flat surface to record notes as they view their sources. They should complete one of these for each video, photo archive, website, or multimedia source they consult.

   - Lead students through the chart, linking the bulleted points below the chart with the highlighted handwritten comments.

2. For the **Source Title**: Use the Title to categorize and organize your research. For untitled media, students should create one of their own that helps identify the content: *Mesoamerican Civilizations.*

3. For the **Viewing Task**, have students record:

   - where they found the source and its format: *PowerPoint Presentation; www.sacramento.k12.ca.us/divdept/sscience/CReview6_8/7Mesoamerica.ppt*

   - how it was accessed and any special pathway or chain needed for access: *Searched Mesoamerican Indians, then linked to PowerPoint on Mayan Civilizations.*

   - whether all of it was used and, if not, what was skipped: *Used Mayan only slides 1-12, Incan, Olmec, and Aztec still available.*

   - how they plan to use the research: *good art and location photos, useful headings for outline*

4. Point out that there are two viewings indicated. Other viewings may be necessary for fact-filled or complex presentations as well as multiple viewings for different purposes.

5. Encourage students to adapt this chart as needed, tailoring their observations to their topic rather than to those bulleted in the chart.

6. Remind students that this chart may be the easiest way to access information while they are writing their paper because opening up a collection of PowerPoint presentations or a chain of interlinked websites may be time consuming and clumsy.

7. Students should particularly note visuals resources they want to use and should record page numbers, hyperlinks, or other ways to locate them.

Source Title: Viewing Task:		
	First Viewing	**Second Viewing**
What I Saw	• slide 4, good map of Yucatan Peninsula with archeological sites • slide 6, good timeline of Mayan civilization • slide 10, series of photos on excavations at Chichen Itza • slide 12, strong graphic about power structure of Mayan society	• slide 5, hieroglyphs of Mayan rulers and priests • slide 7, explanation and samples of calendar
What I Heard	• slide 2, re-enacted Mayan chants and songs • slide 5, narration of religious beliefs • slide 11, interviews with archeologist, Dr. Selena Veracruz	• slide 1, round table discussion of Mayan achievements • slide 7, examples of modern languages similar to Mayan

8. Once students have isolated the visual resources they want to use in the report they should follow these guidelines for their proper application:

   - Choose photos, illustrations, or other artwork based on their relevance to the material being considered. Don't just include a visual because you think it's cool. Each should have a purpose.

   - Avoid using too many visuals. They should complement the writing and help to illustrate your major points.

   - Use visuals that reinforce or demonstrate the ideas in your writing. Careful selection and intensive research will help you isolate visuals that teach your reader.

   - Use screen captures from websites and videos, or copy and/or drag and drop slides from PowerPoints or storyboards.

   - Place charts or other data presentations as close as possible to a part of the text that discusses them so readers won't have to keep turning pages to reference the data.

   - Be sure to properly credit any photos or information taken from visual resources, citing the source, as you would with any paraphrase or quotation.

   - Students who have computer skills should assist others who are less savvy at accessing and using visual resources via the computer. Students may also need assistance in copying print media sources, too.

9. Assign the independent writing activity.

Reference

Jones, R. *Rigor and Relevance Handbook*. Rexford, NY: International Center for Leadership in Education, 2010.

For the Student

Independent Writing Activity

1. This activity will require students to access — by means of library or online sources — a photo archive or collection as well as a PowerPoint presentation or some other multimedia presentation.

2. As students locate visual resources, have them make strategic use of digital media (e.g., textual, graphical, audio, visual, and interactive elements) in presentations to enhance their understanding of findings, reasoning, and evidence and to add interest to their research.

3. Ask students to think carefully about their topic and research different aspects of it.

4. They should be looking for visual resources that would enhance their presentation. Depending on their topic of their report, students should add all or at least most of the following visual resources:

   - Add photos to illustrate the people, places, and things prominently mentioned in the report.

   - Present graphics, like charts, graphs, tables, models, maps, cutaways, formulas, or various figures to present data or other statistical information.

   - Use artworks, paintings, and photos of sculpture or ancient artifacts to bring life to topics that occurred before the invention of the camera.

   - Adapt parts of PowerPoint or Whiteboard slides.

   - Include screengrabs of videos, movies, or any films. Relevant audio should be transcribed for the reader.

- Provide hyperlinks or web addresses if readers need to consult a visual source further.

- Direct your reader on how to use the visual resources you've found. The visual sources can provide additional information to your report and help convince readers of your argument.

5. Students should explain as part of this assignment how they plan on using visual and audio resources in their work. They should also discuss the impact they feel their visual and audio resources will have on their readers or their viewers.

6. Have the class critique and discuss the effects of the visual and audio media that students have chosen.

7. Answers and visual presentations will vary greatly, but students should be judged on how well they use the media found in their research. The visuals should be more than adornment and help the reader understand the thesis statement as well as the topic sentences of individual paragraphs. They should furthermore act as evidence backing up reasons in arguments, as added description, and as elements of storytelling in narrative writing.

Viewing Notes Chart

Source Title: Viewing Task:		
	First Viewing	**Second Viewing**
What I Saw		
What I Heard		

Main Idea and Relevant Details

Defining the Strategy

Determining the main idea and its supporting details is a challenging fundamental skill that increases reading comprehension; however, as a writing skill, composing the main idea and relevant details is an imposing task that forces writers to determine what they want to say. Clarity is crucial to analytic academic writing and writers must clearly convey different types of main ideas. There is the main idea of the overall work, the larger concepts that make up the topic, the essentials of the writer's claim, as well as the main ideas behind the reasons or evidence that are offered to back the claim. All of these controlling ideas have to work together to give the writing impact and meaning. It doesn't matter which type of academic writing the writer is producing. An argument's claim or thesis is its controlling main idea. Explanatory writing, like all exposition, focuses on central ideas that are then explained as secondary concepts. Even narrative writing has a message or an intended effect that serves as its main idea. And all three of these forms are supported with details that are relevant to the argument, explanation, or story being told.

In order to formulate a main idea, a writer should be able to state it in one concise sentence, or thesis statement. The thesis should contain the core or gist of what the writer wants to say. It is the most important piece of information the author has to share. It should simply answer the question, "What is this about?" The facts that back up the answer to this question are relevant details, which are linked to each other within the argument and related to other truths or observations. Other entertaining or unrelated details may form part of the overall writing, but valid reasoning and relevant and sufficient evidence must support the main idea. The structure of writing helps both the reader and the writer to examine and convey complex ideas and information through the effective selection, organization, and analysis of content.

The construction of a work's main ideas and relevant details is well modeled by the skills matrix on the Rigor/Relevance Framework. Research and basic understanding fall within the Knowledge/Awareness phase and move into Comprehension. As writers formulate their main ideas, they complete Application. In the writing process, they engage in Analysis, Synthesis, and eventually after their work is read, Evaluation.

Applying the Strategy

Writing the main idea and relevant details is an effective strategy in most content areas and in middle and secondary programs.

Middle School

- Science
    - defining the process of investigation in applying the scientific theory
    - explaining multi-stage processes like genetics or reproduction
    - breaking down similar traits to elucidate the organization or classification of living things
- Social Studies
    - describing the structure and success of dynasties or long-standing civilizations
    - determining major ideas behind social change
    - investigating causes of wars
- Math
    - constructing word problems
    - defining steps in an algebraic proof

- ELA
  - writing plot summaries
  - producing book reports
  - enhancing reading comprehension with analysis of detail
  - composing essays or persuasive writing

Secondary School

- Science
  - breaking down lab reports into theory and observational data
  - explaining the function of human anatomy
  - analyzing interactions within an environment
- Social Studies
  - analyzing religious beliefs in different cultures
  - translating historical data into trends
  - interpreting documents and speeches
- Math
  - solving geometric proofs from details
  - determining significant data from graphic representations
  - explaining the logic behind mathematical interpretation of real-life events
- ELA
  - creating how-to manuals and process writing
  - comparing different works within genres by their theme or thesis
  - summarizing poetry
  - analyzing descriptive writing
  - determining correct grammar use

Common Core State Standards

College and Career Readiness Anchor Standards for Writing

Text Types and Purposes

1. Write arguments to support claims in an analysis of substantive topics or texts, using valid reasoning and relevant and sufficient evidence.

2. Write informative/explanatory texts to examine and convey complex ideas and information clearly and accurately through the effective selection, organization, and analysis of content.

3. Write narratives to develop real or imagined experiences or events using effective technique, well-chosen details, and well-structured event sequences.

Production and Distribution of Writing

4. Produce clear and coherent writing in which the development, organization, and style are appropriate to task, purpose, and audience.

5. Develop and strengthen writing as needed by planning, revising, editing, rewriting, or trying a new approach.

Research to Build and Present Knowledge

6. Conduct short as well as more sustained research projects based on focused questions, demonstrating understanding of the subject under investigation.

Teaching the Strategy

Introduce the strategy by explaining that constructing main ideas and relevant details is a matter of proper organization. There are various ways to present the claim or thesis statement of the overall work as well as the topic sentence for individual paragraphs. Different methods impact readers differently.

- **Upfront — Direct.** The most commonly used approach is to get the main idea out right away. This works best with straightforward expository writing. The claim of an argument is often advanced immediately to alert the reader before evidence is presented. However, an obvious assertion in the first sentence can also be less intriguing for the reader and because it is done so often, may make the writing predictable and have less impact on the reader.

- **Secondary — Bury the Lead.** Writers will often begin with an attention grabber. This is a startling fact or amazing tidbit that makes the reader want to continue reading. It is usually not the main idea. Once the writer has the reader interested, the central point can be established and then expanded. It is also used to provide background to the main idea before revealing it.

- **Wrap Up — Big Finish.** This method of organization puts out details and minor ideas first, building a case for an argument or establishing baseline facts for an explanation. For a narration, a writer might describe a setting and set a mood before making a statement of his or her main idea as the big finish.

- **Front and Back — Hammer It Home.** This method puts the main idea at the very start, supplies some added ideas, and then repeats the main idea for emphasis.

- **Implied — Work the Reader.** This is by far the most subtle approach and demands that readers determine the main idea on their own. This can be very effective when the author is trying to lead readers to draw conclusions and make inferences based on information being provided.

Whatever the method, the first step involves organizing your ideas. Basic structure must include:

- **Introductory Paragraphs.** These advance the main idea, give a scope to the topic, explain how the topic will be covered, and reveal how the writer feels about the topic.
- **Transitional Paragraphs.** In these paragraphs, writers build their case, provide relevant and extraneous details, and put meat on the bones of the argument.
- **Summarizing Paragraphs.** Here, the main ideas are restated and drawn into focus with a summary that defines what has just been read.

Often, graphic organizers are useful in planning how to present the main ideas and details:

- **Spider Map.** This graphic organizer allows you to link main ideas to the topic sentence and then list details as well. The advantage to this structure is that it involves a less formal hierarchy of ideas and the writer can rearrange the order of ideas at will.

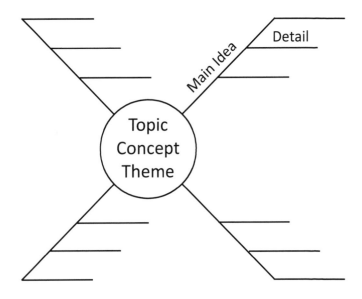

- **Outline Format.** The traditional indented list of ideas ordered by broadest to most detailed with numbers and letters remains the best way to create balanced structure for a written work. Students should adjust the layout to match their topic and ideas.

Main Idea and Details Outline

Title: _____

Subject: _____

Thesis Statement: _____

  I. (Main Idea #1: Topic Sentence) _____

     A. (Relevant Details) _____

     B. _____

     C. _____

 II. (Main Idea #2: Topic Sentence) _____

     A. (Relevant Details) _____

     B. _____

     C. _____

III. (Main Idea #3: Topic Sentence) _____

     A. (Relevant Details) _____

     B. _____

     C. _____

    Conclusion: _____

    _____

Directed Writing Activity

1. This activity will require students to produce clear and coherent writing in which development, organization, and style are appropriate to task and purpose. Use the main ideas and relevant details supplied here to fill in one or both of the graphic organizers.

2. As appropriate to your class and the topic, copy and distribute either the spider map or the outline graphic organizer, or allow students to choose one and create it themselves.

3. Ask students to read the following excerpt from a government report about restoring grizzly bears to wilderness areas. They should use this information as research to plan and outline their report.

4. Students should isolate main ideas and relevant details in the text and then record them in the outline graphic organizer while you demonstrate.

5. Begin with the title and subject and have students make suggestions for each. They should try to summarize the article in a few words.

6. Leave the topic sentence blank until you have considered the main ideas. Main Idea #1 should be formulated from the research, but ask students to restate the ideas as they would write them in their own report.

7. Be sure to point out to students how the details are relevant to the main ideas.

8. Once the main ideas and details are recorded, go back and formulate a thesis statement. Remind students that it needs to encapsulate the main ideas and act as the main claim for the argument.

9. After learners complete their graphic organizers, review and discuss the assignment. Encourage students to describe the organizers they used and why they chose them. Ask students to explain their choices for main ideas, why the details were relevant, and how their thesis statement matches the research.

10. Assign the independent writing activity.

Reference

Jones, R. *Using Rigor and Relevance to Create Effective Instruction*. Rexford, NY: International Center for Leadership in Education, 2012.

Sample Report Research

The Fish and Wildlife Service of the Department of Interior intends to re-establish the threatened grizzly bear in the Bitterroot ecosystem. Grizzly bears are a part of America's rich wildlife heritage and once ranged throughout most of the western United States. However, distribution and population levels of this species have been diminished by excessive human-caused mortality and loss of habitat. Today, only 1,000 to 1,100 grizzly bears remain in a few populations in four western states.

Wildlife species, like grizzly bear, are most vulnerable when confined to small portions of their historical range and limited to a few, small populations. Expansion of the range of the species will increase the number of bears within the lower 48 United States, increase habitat size and extent, and further conservation of the species. The Bitterroot ecosystem is one of the largest contiguous blocks of Federal land remaining in the lower 48 United States. The core of the ecosystem contains two wilderness areas, which comprise the largest block of wilderness habitat in the Rocky Mountains south of Canada. Of all remaining unoccupied grizzly bear habitat in the lower 48 States, this area in the Bitterroot Mountains has the best potential for grizzly bear recovery, primarily due to the large wilderness area. As such, the Bitterroot ecosystem offers excellent potential to support a healthy population of grizzly bears and to boost long-term survival and recovery prospects for this species in the contiguous United States.

Having made the above findings, the Service has decided to proceed, as funding permits, with implementation of the Proposed Action Alternative. The decision to implement this alternative is subject to the following conditions that will further minimize or avoid the environmental impacts and public concerns identified during the environmental review process:

(1) The process of grizzly bear recovery in the Bitterroot ecosystem will be implemented in a staged process with initial formation of the Citizen Management Committee (CMC), and ongoing sanitation enhancement and public information efforts; (2) if the Service receives adequate funding, grizzly bears could be reintroduced in 2002, following formation of the CMC and successful initiation of the sanitation and informational efforts, which will be ongoing as the bears are placed in the area; (3) bears for reintroduction will be taken from areas more than 10 miles beyond existing recovery zone lines in the Yellowstone and NorthernContinental Divide ecosystems, and from British Columbia and Alaska (nonsalmon-eating bears), as appropriate; (4) to maximize human safety and bear survival, bears placed in the Bitterroot will have no history of conflict with people or livestock; (5) all reintroduced bears will be radio-monitored upon placement; and (6) at least 25 bears will be placed into the area in coordination with the CMC and this number may increase pending scientific considerations of the need to have a larger initial population so as to increase the probability of eventual recovery. (From http://www.gpo.gov/fdsys/pkg/FR-2000-11-17/pdf/00-29531)

Sample Outline

Title: Bringing Grizzly Bears Back to the West

Subject: Reintroduction of grizzly bears to wilderness areas in the western United States

Thesis Statement: In order to save endangered grizzly bears, our government must bring bears into a large wilderness area and take precautions to help the bears repopulate without threatening humans.

I. Grizzly bears need to be reintroduced and established in the western United States.

    A. Grizzly bears once ranged throughout most of the western United States.

    B. Excessive human-caused mortality and loss of habitat has reduced their distribution and population.

    C. Only 1,000 to 1,100 grizzly bears remain in a few populations in four western states.

II. Grizzly bears will be brought into the Bitterroot ecosystem because it is the best place for them to repopulate.

    A. Grizzly bears are vulnerable when small populations are confined in limited areas.

    B. The Bitterroot ecosystem contains two large wilderness areas, which comprise the largest block of wilderness habitat south of Canada.

    C. Bitterroot ecosystem offers excellent potential to support a healthy population of grizzly bears and to boost long-term survival and recovery prospects for this species.

III. The Service will go ahead with the grizzly bear reintroduction but will take certain precautions so the proposal will be successful.

    A. Bears will be introduced slowly in stages and the public will be well informed.

    B. The grizzly bears that are brought in will be taken from truly wild areas and will not have any history of conflicts with humans.

    C. All 25 re-introduced bears will be radio-monitored and more bears will be added to increase the probability of eventual recovery.

Conclusion: Grizzly bears should be able to repopulate the Bitterroot ecosystem as long as they are kept away from the human population of the surrounding area.

For the Student

Independent Writing Activity

Use one of the graphic organizers to prepare an outline of your structure for another type of analytical academic paper. Develop your writing appropriately by planning, revising, and editing.

1. If research materials are available, draw from these materials to formulate a topic sentence as well as main ideas and relevant details.

2. If you are not able to research, create an outline for a narrative report. This would be a story or a series of personal observation on any topic you choose. Select something you know well and can recall from memory.

3. Complete a graphic organizer that fully describes a narrative you would write. It should be about real or imagined experiences or events and you should use effective technique, well-chosen details, and well-structured event sequences.

4. If time allows, compose a narrative using the outline.

Spider Map

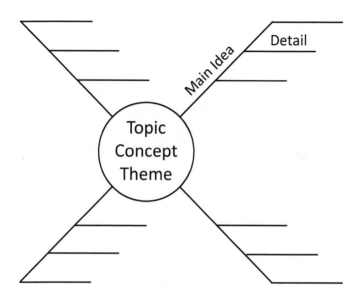

Main Ideas and Details Outline

Title: _____

Subject: _____

Thesis Statement: _____

I. (Main Idea #1: Topic Sentence) _____

    A. (Relevant Details) _____

    B. _____

    C. _____

II. (Main Idea #2: Topic Sentence) _____

    A. (Relevant Details) _____

    B. _____

    C. _____

III. (Main Idea #3: Topic Sentence) _____

    A. (Relevant Details) _____

    B. _____

    C. _____

Conclusion: _____

_____

■ Minute Paper

Defining the Strategy

In the Minute Paper strategy, students respond to a literary or informational text by writing about the text in just a few short minutes. This is an effective way to help them focus on key points in a text and reflect on new information to connect reading with learning. The technique teaches students to analyze the writing purpose, identify the audience, and organize evidence from the text. It guides students to identify main ideas and frame questions that the reading raised but did not answer. It is also an excellent way for students to prepare for assessments that require them to construct written responses to specific prompts on a variety of topics.

The Minute Paper strategy may fall in Quadrants B or C in the Rigor/Relevance framework, depending on the complexity of the text and any writing prompt. If a student is asked to read, respond to, and question an assigned literary or informational text, this activity would fall in Quadrant B. If a student is asked to read, analyze, synthesize, or evaluate information from the text, this would fall in Quadrant C.

Applying the Strategy

This strategy aligns with standards 1 and 9 of the Common Core College and Career Anchor Standards for Writing. Standard 1 focuses on writing arguments. A minute paper is an excellent way to record initial reactions "on paper." A minute paper can also serve as the steppingstone from which to write an argument paper.

Anchor standard 8 focuses on gathering relevant information from multiple sources and integrating that information while avoiding plagiarism. A minute paper would be particularly useful for students working on a research paper or project. It will provide good practice for students in writing information in their own words.

Anchor standard 9 requires students to draw evidence from texts to support analysis, reflection, and research. A Minute Paper is an excellent way for students to see what they remember or what resonates with them from a text. By reading a text and then immediately writing about the text in a given amount of time, ideas that resonate with students will appear in their Minute Paper.

Minute Paper writing is an effective strategy in most content areas in middle and secondary programs.

Middle School

- Science
  - learning key details of scientific concepts such as structure and function in living systems, the structure of the Earth system, and adaptations of organisms
- Social Studies
  - summarizing main points of historical time periods and events
  - analyzing political and economic systems
- Math
  - understanding mathematical concepts and processes

- ELA
  - understanding main ideas
  - asking questions

Secondary School

- Science
  - summarizing key information such as the structure and properties of matter and the interdependence and behavior of organisms
- Social Studies
  - listing the physical and human characteristics of places
  - summarizing how human actions modify the physical environment
- Math
  - listing the rules of exponents
  - understanding similarity and how it can be proven
- ELA
  - understanding main ideas and details
  - asking questions
  - analyzing text

Common Core State Standards

College and Career Readiness Anchor

Text Types and Purposes

2. Write informative/explanatory texts to examine and convey complex ideas and information clearly and accurately through the effective selection, organization, and analysis of content.

onal Strategies for Content-Area Writing 7–12

Production and Distribution of Writing

4. Produce clear and coherent writing in which the development, organization, and style are appropriate to task, purpose, and audience.

Research to Build and Present Knowledge

9. Draw evidence from literary or informational texts to support analysis, reflection, and research.

Range of Writing

10. Write routinely over extended time frames (time for research, reflection, and revision) and shorter time frames (a single sitting or a day or two) for a range of tasks, purposes, and audiences.

Teaching the Strategy

Introduce the Minute Paper strategy by explaining that it can be used for many purposes.

- **To identify.** The Minute Paper strategy is useful for identifying main ideas and key details in the text.

- **To generate.** This strategy is effective for generating questions about the text that will help students increase their understanding through reflection.

- **To apply.** The Minute Paper strategy, when used with technical or informational texts, can help students apply facts and ideas in the text to the world outside the classroom.

- **To predict.** A Minute Paper exercise can be used to prompt students to predict outcomes in a literary text.

- **To analyze.** This strategy, when used with a writing prompt, aids students in analyzing texts. Student will reinforce their ability to use reasoning as well as relevant and sufficient evidence to support a viewpoint.

To assist students in writing a Minute Paper, introduce the Focus Areas Chart. Explain that they should think about these focus areas as they read. However, they should not write in the chart as they read. They should spend their time focusing on what they are reading. The Focus Areas Chart is divided into 3 sections: Significant Points, Unanswered Questions, and Ah-has for Application.

Significant points consist of main ideas and key terms. Unanswered questions are questions students still need to answer or would like answered about the topic. Ah-has for application are new ideas and ideas for how to apply what they read to other real-world areas.

Significant Points	Unanswered Questions	Ah-has for Application

Directed Writing Activity

1. Assign students an article or chapter to read. It should be no longer than they can reasonably read in one sitting. If you want to assign a full-length work, divide it into chapters or short sections and have students write a Minute Paper for each chapter or section as they progress through the entire book.

2. Give each student a copy of the Focus Areas Chart.

3. Have students read the assigned text silently. Remind them not to take notes as they read.

4. You may choose to have students discuss the reading with partners before they begin writing their Minute Papers. Discussion should concentrate on the most significant points in the reading and any unanswered questions. If the reading consists of one chapter of a full-length work, partners can discuss predictions

about later chapters. If the reading is informational, partners can discuss any real-world applications they have identified.

5. Model the process of writing a Minute Paper for students. Think aloud as you do so to demonstrate the process fully. Have students keep track of the time and tell you when 5 minutes have passed. Allow students to discuss and ask questions about your modeled Minute Paper.

6. After a short discussion period, direct students to write their own Minute Papers. They may use the lower portion of their organizer or a sheet of blank paper to record their responses. Warn students that they will only be given five minutes to write; therefore they must concentrate on the most important ideas or details from the assigned reading. Inform students of when their five minutes begins and ends.

7. Use the Minute Papers as a basis for class discussion of the reading. If the reading consists of a chapter of a longer work, encourage students to continue reading to find the answers to their questions.

8. After students complete their Minute Papers, review and discuss the assignment. Discuss specifically the effect that only having five minutes had on their writing.

9. As an additional activity, have students write a Minute Paper on the same selection, but using a specific writing prompt, such as "How did you feel about . . . " "What surprised you most . . . ," and so on.

10. Assign the independent writing activity.

For the Student

Independent Writing Activity

Follow these directions to write a Minute Paper. Remember, you will only have five minutes. The purpose is not to produce finished writing, but to focus on your understanding of the reading selection. Your Minute Paper should address key terms and main ideas. It should bring up any questions that the reading suggested to you but didn't answer.

1. Read the text provided.

2. Use your Minute Paper organizer to focus on the following areas as you read:

   - **Main idea.** What is the main idea of the assigned reading? What are the key supporting details?

   - **Unanswered questions.** Now that you've read the selection, what questions do you still have? What new questions do you have?

   - **Application.** How does the text apply to the real world?

3. Discuss the focus areas listed in Step 2 with your reading partner.

4. When your teacher says "Go," take five minutes to complete the focus areas chart and use that information to write a response.

5. Exchange Minute Papers with your partner. Compare key points, questions, and real-world applications or predictions and conclusions. Take part in a class discussion of the assigned reading.

Sample Focus Areas Chart

Significant Points	Unanswered Questions	Ah-has for Application
• U.S. may be target of agro-terrorism. • Animals and crops are subject to diseases. • People can get sick from eating diseased animals.	• How can terrorists infect animals and crops? • Have terrorists ever succeeded in such an attack?	• Restaurant and market owners want to know that the food they serve and sell is safe for their customers.

My Minute Paper

I learned from this article that the U.S. food supply is subject to attacks. The article says that livestock and crops can be diseased or infected, and that when people eat this food, they can get sick. An attack like this could affect millions of people. This makes me question how any organization could actually make such an attack. Would it be enough to infect one animal? How could a terrorist get access to a livestock animal, or to a plant that processes food?

There are lots of businesses that would be concerned about the safety of the food supply. People who own and operate markets, grocery stores, and restaurants have to be able to assure their customers that the food they sell and prepare is safe to eat. These industry people might become a powerful political lobby that could keep the food safe for all of us.

Agricultural Terrorism

In 2003, the discovery of a single cow with bovine enceph-alopathy, better known as mad cow disease, crippled the Canadian cattle market. In 2002, the mere rumor of foot-and-mouth disease in Kansas sent shock waves through the American cattle industry. The discovery of exotic New-castle disease in southern California led to the destruction of millions of chickens and prompted many countries to ban poultry coming from the area.

Agriculture and homeland security officials cite these and similar events in describing the possible effects of a bio-terror attack on domestic agriculture. Officials take such threats seriously; the terrorist group Al Qaeda years ago put the U.S. food supply on its list of potential targets. The federal government is working to bolster the nation's readiness for an agro-terror attack.

From farm crops and animals through the processing sys-tem to the grocery store, the food supply chain provides numerous opportunities for attack. Moreover, the sys-tem would ensure rapid disease progression: animals are moved often and quickly, and anti-crop agents can be spread by the wind. Since the terrorist attacks of Septem-ber 11, 2001, the U.S. Department of Agriculture has hired new inspectors and strengthened its diagnostic capabili-ties around the country. The Food and Drug Administra-tion has bolstered food safety rules and made it easier for investigators to trace the origins of an outbreak.

Focus Areas Chart

Significant Points	Unanswered Questions	Ah-has for Application

My Minute Paper

▟ Paraphrasing

Defining the Strategy

The word *paraphrase* comes from Greek, meaning "alongside" and "to show or explain." A writer needs to paraphrase in order to show or explain something by sharing the ideas of others with words that are not the same but which are freshly stated, as well as identical in meaning, like train tracks running alongside each other. A good paraphrase is a restatement of what a writer has read, including both main ideas and relevant details. It is not a summary, which only retells the main idea of a passage.

When you are researching a topic and taking notes, it is not always practical or wise to constantly copy quotations. Using the exact words of others robs writers of their own voices. Instead, if writers read a quote carefully, fully understand it, then reform it in their own words, they have successfully processed the ideas (without plagiarism) and as long as they cite their sources, they can lay claim to a fresh thought. In the process of writing analytical academic work, writers need to synthesize what they have learned without merely listing the quotations of other thinkers.

For a writer, paraphrasing is an extension of your research that demands higher orders of thinking, not just mechanical regurgitation of the words and thoughts of other writers. You need to read closely to determine what the text says explicitly and to make logical inferences from it. This means fully understanding what was written, interpreting words and phrases as they are used in a text. As you paraphrase, you determine central ideas or themes of a text and analyze their development and consequently reconsider the key supporting details and ideas. Whenever you paraphrase, however, avoid plagiarism or overreliance on any one source. In addition, follow a standard format for citation.

Paraphrasing begins within Quadrant A on the Rigor/Relevance Framework with basic research. The decision of how to use a quotation falls within Quadrant B as students recompose what they have read and apply the appropriate knowledge to a new situation. The paraphrase itself becomes a unique solution as students think in complex ways, particularly as they synthesize knowledge from another source and repurpose it for their own uses.

Applying the Strategy

Paraphrasing is an effective writing strategy in most content areas and in middle and secondary programs.

Middle School

- Science
  - recreating well-known lab procedures
  - quoting famous scientists and their writings
  - restating basic scientific theories and laws of nature
- Social Studies
  - translating archaic or hard to understand primary source materials to modern language
  - citing the works of others in researching the works of historians through different eras
  - quoting famous people's opinions

- Math
  - recreating word problems
  - quoting mathematical theories
- ELA
  - abbreviating larger passages of fiction
  - composing a research paper from various experts in a genre or literary movement

Secondary School

- Science
  - quoting or paraphrasing research in the field
  - citing theories from researchers
  - composing a research paper that uses the work of others as a starting point
- Social Studies
  - paraphrasing letters and memoirs of historical figures
  - condensing extensively detailed records of a period
- Math
  - citing sources while researching significant figures in the history of mathematics
  - repeating proofs and explanations from various sources
- ELA
  - interpreting a survey of different theories about an author's work
  - quoting from author interviews or reviews
  - paraphrasing segments too long to quote from the original

Common Core State Standards

College and Career Readiness Anchor Standards for Writing

Text Types and Purposes

1. Write arguments to support claims in an analysis of substantive topics or texts, using valid reasoning and relevant and sufficient evidence.

2. Write informative/explanatory texts to examine and convey complex ideas and information clearly and accurately through the effective selection, organization, and analysis of content.

3. Write narratives to develop real or imagined experiences or events using effective technique, well-chosen details, and well-structured event sequences.

Production and Distribution of Writing

4. Produce clear and coherent writing in which the development, organization, and style are appropriate to task, purpose, and audience.

5. Develop and strengthen writing as needed by planning, revising, editing, rewriting, or trying a new approach.

Research to Build and Present Knowledge

7. Conduct short as well as more sustained research projects based on focused questions, demonstrating understanding of the subject under investigation.

8. Gather relevant information from multiple print and digital sources, assess the credibility and accuracy of each source, and integrate the information while avoiding plagiarism.

9. Draw evidence from literary or informational texts to support analysis, reflection, and research.

Teaching the Strategy

Introduce the strategy by explaining that paraphrasing is a skill that must be practiced and that there are proven techniques that will produce strong paraphrasing.

- **Read carefully without copying anything.** Read the original until you can follow the ideas in your head. Then set the quote aside and restate the ideas, not the sentences in the same form. You can change the order of presentation, and the way of saying it, but still have the same ideas.

- **Break the quote down.** Particularly for longer quotations, break up the ideas into segments that can be rewritten with different words and moved around if necessary.

- **Cite the source.** Jot down the page number and any ideas you may have as to how to use the ideas or how they are related to other ideas. These will make it easier to use when you are writing.

- **Quote unique words or phrases.** Sometimes you shouldn't change the words, particularly for an effective turn of a phrase or a clever term. Once properly attributed or quoted you can use it again and again without quotes for effect.

- **Double check the original.** Make sure you got the ideas right. Sometimes, restating an idea twists connections around. You want to be certain you grasp what you've just said.

As an example, have students read the passage that follows and then the proper paraphrase followed by a plagiarized paraphrase and then a confused paraphrase. Work through the text sentence-by-sentence, idea-by-idea, to have students see how it is properly done.

- **Original Text** (from President Kennedy's Inaugural Address): "We dare not forget today that we are the heirs of that first revolution. Let the word go forth from this time and place, to friend and foe alike, that the torch has been passed to a new generation of Americans — born in this century, tempered by war, disciplined by a hard and bitter peace, proud of our ancient heritage — and unwilling to witness or permit the slow undoing of those human rights to which this Nation has always been committed, and to which we are committed today at home and around the world."

- **Proper Paraphrase:** We must remember that all of us are related to those who fought for our freedom from Great Britain. I am right here and now declaring that the young people of this nation will carry on the traditions of our revolution. They are young, tested by war and peace, and respect their ancestors. They refuse to stand by and watch anyone take away their rights. Our country fought for those rights and we are all ready to fight for those rights against anyone who would deny them to us.

- **Plagiarized Paraphrase:** We shouldn't forget today that we are heirs of the Revolutionary War. Let the word get out from this place and time, to friends and foes, that a new generation in America will carry the torch. They were born in this century, survived a war, and have been disciplined by a bitter peace and are proud of our heritage, but they are unwilling to stand by and watch or allow someone undoing their human rights for which their nation has always been committed, and we are still committed to those things today at home and all over the world.

- **Confused Paraphrase:** We are the daring heirs of a revolution. Let everyone spread the word to our friends and those who are like our foes, that a new American generation has passed a torch that was born one hundred years ago and went through a war, teaching the rules of a difficult and nasty peace but still proud of being ancient with a heritage and unwilling to be a witness or permit anyone doing anything to our human rights. Our nation should be committed and we are committed to it today even at home and all over the world.

Directed Writing Activity

1. For this activity use the Paraphrasing Matrix shown below to break down the different paraphrases in the sample.

2. Refer to the italicized comments in the Original column on the left, which comments on the relative strengths or weaknesses of each paraphrase. Help students see how the Proper paraphrase retains the original meaning while the Plagiarized one just lifts the words without any reinterpretation and the Confused one distorts the meaning.

Original: We dare not forget today that we are the heirs of that first revolution. *(Note that the Proper links the audience to the past but the Confused gets it wrong and the Plagiarized is too close.)*	Proper: We must remember that all of us are related to those who fought for our freedom from Great Britain.
	Plagiarized: We shouldn't forget today that we are heirs of the Revolutionary War.
	Confused: We are the daring heirs of a revolution.
Original: Let the word go forth from this time and place, to friend and foe alike, that the torch has been passed to a new generation of Americans *(Note that the Proper translates the phrase "the torch has been passed" as "carry on the traditions" with the meaning intact. The Confused blurs "alike" and has the torch passed by the new generation not passed "to them.")*	Proper: I am right here and now declaring that the young people of this nation will carry on the traditions of our revolution.
	Plagiarized: Let the word get out from this place and time, to friends and foes, that a new generation in America will carry the torch.
	Confused: Let everyone spread the word to our friends and those who are like our foes, that a new American generation has passed a torch

Original:—born in this century, tempered by war, disciplined by a hard and bitter peace, proud of our ancient heritage— *(The Proper defines the same qualities but with a fresh take; the Plagiarized changes a few words but still says the exact same thing; the Confused is talking about the torch not the generation.)*	**Proper:** They are young, tested by war and peace, and respect their ancestors.
	Plagiarized: They were born in this century, survived a war, and have been disciplined by a bitter peace and are proud of our heritage,
	Confused: that was born one hundred years ago and went through a war, teaching the rules of a difficult and nasty peace but still proud of being ancient with a heritage
Original: and unwilling to witness or permit the slow undoing of those human rights to which this Nation has always been committed, *(The Proper focuses on the rights this new generation and older generations fought for; the Plagiarized uses synonyms but not for the key terms; the Confused uses "a witness" for "to witness" and makes it seem like our nation is crazy.)*	**Proper:** They refuse to stand by and watch anyone take away their rights. Our country fought for those rights
	Plagiarized: But they are unwilling to stand by and watch or allow someone undoing their human rights for which their nation has always been committed,
	Confused: and unwilling to be a witness or permit anyone doing anything to our human rights. Our nation should be committed
Original: and to which we are committed today at home and around the world. *(The Proper interprets the commitment to rights without putting it the same way; the Confused shifts from our rights to "it" without the same defense against everyone.)*	**Proper:** and we are all ready to fight for those rights against anyone who would deny them to us.
	Plagiarized: and we are still committed to those things today at home and all over the world.
	Confused: and we are committed to it today even at home and all over the world.

3. Review the following rules for paraphrasing.
   - Attribute it to the original source.
   - Make it shorter than the original.
   - Use your words but express the ideas properly.
   - Link your work to the work of others.
   - Use a quote when changing the words would lose something important.
   - Paraphrase if the quote is too long or hard to understand or if you are blending it with other ideas.
4. Assign the independent writing activity.

Reference

Jones, R. *Rigor and Relevance Handbook*. Rexford, NY: International Center for Leadership in Education, 2010.

For the Student

Independent Writing Activity

Follow these directions to write proper paraphrases of the original passages. Develop your writing appropriately by planning, revising, and editing.

1. Carefully read the following copy of President Abraham Lincoln's Gettysburg Address and the excerpt from the Declaration of Independence.

2. Treat it as researched source material for a report. Create paraphrases of the major ideas using modern language for a modern audience.

3. Complete the blank Paraphrasing Matrix provided. Note that the original text should be inserted on the left and your paraphrase entered on the right.

4. Use quotes if necessary for words or phrases you wish to keep in the original form.

5. Write a paragraph for each passage, discussing the ideas that they contain. Express your own opinion or place these ideas into the context of the horrors of the Civil War or the need for our country to be free of the tyranny of Great Britain. Use your basic knowledge of these historical events to help you.

Student paraphrasing will vary greatly but should contain the major ideas of each work and use modern language. Students can use the ideas in a variety of ways but should mix their paraphrasing of the original ideas in with direct quotations, while discussing the basics of the Civil War and the start of the Revolutionary War.

Gettysburg Address

Four score and seven years ago, our fathers brought forth on this continent a new nation: conceived in liberty, and dedicated to the proposition that all men are created equal. Now we are engaged in a great civil war . . . testing whether that nation, or any nation so conceived and so dedicated . . . can long endure. We are met on a great battlefield of that war. We have come to dedicate a portion of that field as a final resting place for those who here gave their lives that that nation might live. It is altogether fitting and proper that we should do this. But, in a larger sense, we cannot dedicate . . . we cannot consecrate . . . we cannot hallow this ground. The brave men, living and dead, who struggled here have consecrated it, far above our poor power to add or detract. The world will little note, nor long remember, what we say here, but it can never forget what they did here. It is for us the living, rather, to be dedicated here to the unfinished work which they who fought here have thus far so nobly advanced.   It is rather for us to be here dedicated to the great task remaining before us . . . that from these honored dead we take increased devotion to that cause for which they gave the last full measure of devotion . . . that we here highly resolve that these dead shall not have died in vain . . . that this nation, under God, shall have a new birth of freedom . . . and that government of the people . . . by the people . . . for the people . . . shall not perish from the earth.

from the Declaration of Independence

When, in the course of human events, it becomes necessary for one people to dissolve the political bands which have connected them with another, and to assume among the powers of the earth, the separate and equal station to which the laws of nature and of nature's God entitle them, a decent respect to the opinions of mankind requires that they should declare the causes which impel them to the separation. We hold these truths to be self-evident, that all men are created equal, that they are endowed by their Creator with certain unalienable rights, that among these are life, liberty and the pursuit of happiness.—That to secure these rights, governments are instituted among men, deriving their just powers from the consent of the governed.—That whenever any form of government becomes destructive to these ends, it is the right of the people to alter or to abolish it, and to institute new government, laying its foundation on such principles and organizing its powers in such form, as to them shall seem most likely to effect their safety and happiness.

Paraphrasing Matrix

Original	Paraphrase

 RAFT

For the Teacher

Defining the Strategy

When facing a writing task, the average student needs starting points, encouraging prompts, and solid organizational framework in order to answer the question, "What am I supposed to write?" To require a student with weak writing skills to come up with a topic or claim, a working structure, and an appropriate voice focused on an audience is a tall order. One helpful strategy known as RAFT (Role, Audience, Format, Topic) provides students with supports, prompts, and guidance in much the same way a blow-up inflatable raft keeps you from sinking in unfamiliar water. The RAFT strategy first asks students to examine the *role* that they are taking on in a piece of writing. Students can, for instance, write as themselves, but the RAFT strategy also encourages students to try on a variety of roles — everything from a character in history or literature to an underappreciated punctuation mark, like the semicolon. Once writers choose their role, the RAFT strategy asks them to think concretely about the *audience* to whom they are writing, the *format* they will use, and the *topic* they will cover.

As both a strategy and a form, RAFT combines the task of writing with the activity of reading. After students have studied a topic, RAFT helps them achieve a deeper understanding of the text by using what they have learned. They learn to write from the perspective of the people, places, and things about which they have just been reading. The RAFT strategy is a task students can perform in groups or individually, and they can design their own RAFT assignment if they wish. It also encourages young writers to experiment with different formats, voices, and writing approaches while stimulating their creativity and imagination in order to reach audiences beyond their teachers or fellow students. As a written form of role-playing, it opens the door to a fresh approach that goes beyond the often sterile or dry essay format. At the same time, it helps writers avoid completely unstructured, free-for-all creative writing.

The RAFT strategy is often quite effective in helping students increase their comprehension of the research they have done — using multiple print and digital sources — for a formal academic essay or theme/term paper. Because RAFT encourages students to write in a variety of formats, it demands a different type of analytical writing. RAFT is also well suited to narrative writing, since it has students think from unique perspectives and step outside their narrow world view and voice in order to develop real or imagined experiences or events using effective technique and well-chosen details. RAFT also requires students to examine and convey complex ideas and information through the effective selection, organization, and analysis of content. In particular, RAFT is effective at developing and strengthening writing as needed because it gives students practice in planning, revising, editing, rewriting, or trying a new approach.

Because DSEI emphasizes student-focused activities, RAFT writing strategies provide the perfect blend of flexible structures that support student-driven performance while simultaneously allowing teachers to facilitate learning. The writing results can be assessed in a variety of ways. Moreover, because of RAFT's proven success in teaching creative writing as well as its popularity with students, it represents a functional best practice to emulate. RAFT also demands creativity and imagination as a higher expectation for the beginning writer, since it allows students to write as they learn and reuse what they have learned.

Applying the Strategy

RAFT is an effective strategy in most content areas and in middle and secondary programs.

Middle School

- Science
    - imagining the roles of each part of an ecosystem
    - discussing the various processes at work in cycles like the rock or nitrogen cycles
- Social Studies
    - exploring why world leaders made impossible decisions like dropping the atom bomb on Japan
    - understanding why nations become longtime allies or enemies
- Math
    - applying definitions and properties of integers to new applications
    - imagining relationships between real world phenomena and mathematical notations
- ELA
    - discussing how characters from one story would behave in another story
    - delving into the relationships between grammatical concepts
    - creating characters in fiction
    - determining the audience for book reviews
    - exploring the features of various writing formats

Secondary School

- Science
    - understanding an animal's role in evolution or the classification system
    - revealing the inner workings of complex systems like human anatomy, computer technology, or nature

- Social Studies
  - walking a mile in the shoes of our ancestors
  - appreciating why a long-established power eventually fails
  - bringing historical moments to life
- Math
  - exploring relationships between seemingly disparate concepts like square roots and whole numbers
  - discussing tools we all use — such as ratio, scale, function — and how they make tasks easier
  - explaining connections between 2- or 3-dimensional figures
- ELA
  - exploring writing formats not normally attempted in school
  - imagining what lesser characters would be like if expanded
  - practicing creative use of descriptive words and phrases

Common Core State Standards

College and Career Readiness Anchor Standards for Writing

Text Types and Purposes

1. Write arguments to support claims in an analysis of substantive topics or texts, using valid reasoning and relevant and sufficient evidence.

2. Write informative/explanatory texts to examine and convey complex ideas and information clearly and accurately through the effective selection, organization, and analysis of content.

3. Write narratives to develop real or imagined experiences or events using effective technique, well-chosen details, and well-structured event sequences.

Production and Distribution of Writing

4. Produce clear and coherent writing in which the development, organization, and style are appropriate to task, purpose, and audience.

5. Develop and strengthen writing as needed by planning, revising, editing, rewriting, or trying a new approach.

Research to Build and Present Knowledge

8. Draw evidence from literary or informational texts to support analysis, reflection, and research.

Teaching the Strategy

1. Introduce the strategy by explaining that the acronym RAFT stands for three different prompts. Share these with the class and stress that for every writing task, writers consider these crucial elements:

   - **Role.** Who is the writer? Are you a lawyer, the president, a soldier, a lizard, or a pebble? A writer's role also includes a point of view and a function. Are you a witness to an event or someone leading the charge?

   - **Audience.** Who will be reading this? Will it be the school board, characters in a novel, other forces of nature, or animal babies in the zoo? Remember that your understanding of who is reading will determine what you say and how you say it.

   - **Format.** What format are you using? A newspaper article, business letter, song, public speech, journal entry, email, or brochure? You have to adjust your writing to the type of writing you are using.

   - **Topic.** What are you writing about? Are you describing how to survive as a cave man or how a pebble passes through the heart of a volcano? Your subject has to be something you have done or know about and you should be trying to make a point.

2. Sometimes S is added to RAFT to focus the topic:
   - **Strong Verb:** Do you want to persuade, evaluate, plead, demand, predict, argue, compare, analyze, defend?
3. A RAFT assignment uses a template like the one that follows.

RAFT Writing Template

Role	Audience
Format	Topic
Writing Piece	

4. Students select, or are assigned, a RAFT from an assignment chart like the one following. They then complete the Raft writing template.

RAFT Assignment

Unit/Theme:		Language/Level:	
Role	Audience	Format	Topic

RAFT Rules

- Early on, clearly define your **Role** as writer so the audience knows who you are and why you are writing from a position of authority.

- Indicate to whom you are writing. Let the **Audience** know you are writing to impress them and tailor what you have to say to that audience alone.

- Follow the conventions of the **Format** you are assigned. Use the advantages and limitations of the type of writing to tailor your message.

- Stick to the **Topic** and address it directly. Keep in mind that your role and format will determine how you present your topic and that you must always keep your audience in mind. But you can also show your creativity and imagination in covering the topic with a fresh approach and a strong display of what you know about the subject matter.

Directed Writing Activity

1. Divide the class into small groups and try to blend stronger writers with those still finding their way. Also mingle creative writers with more practically minded writers. Realize that some of your strongest writers may struggle with such a creative exercise.

2. Display the following RAFT chart. Explain that the class will do the assignment together, and then each group will complete a RAFT assignment by themselves.

3. Ask students to brainstorm possible approaches to each of the elements in the RAFT assignment.

4. Write the following sentence on the whiteboard, chalkboard, or overhead projector. Explain that this is how they will restate their assignment.

    You are a judge (Role) who thinks the jury does not understand how to reach a fair decision. You write a biographical sketch (Format) to your jury (Audience) about another judge you know who long ago advised (Strong Verb) you how to judge cases fairly (Topic) based on lessons learned during life.

Role	Audience	Format	Topic	Strong Verb
Judge	Jury	Biographical sketch	How I judge cases fairly	Advise

5. Begin by discussing the judge's point of view (*first person*) and what kind of person the judge might be (*gruff, no nonsense*), and then write a sentence that shows this:

    I have been a judge ever since I was a little boy who had no problem telling my friends when they were wrong or right.

6. Now discuss how to introduce the jury (*lecture*) and what type of an *audience* they may be (*too lenient, soft*). Create a sentence that matches this decision.

You are a group of strangers who never had to decide if a person was guilty and you're thinking that punishing someone for crime is a hard thing to do.

7. Complete the process with both *format* and *topic* by discussing what goes into a biographic sketch *(a short review of another person's life)* and how to handle the topic *(advise the jury to follow the examples found in the life of another person).*

Let me tell you a story about my father who was a judge. He learned the hard way how to judge someone fairly. He rode a horse from town to town hearing cases, and one day he heard a case about a horse thief who was such a nice fellow that everyone in town swore he couldn't have done such a thing. So my father let him off, being a firm believer in the goodness of men, and the next morning, his horse was gone and the horse thief rode off to Mexico on it. So, don't let someone's personality fool you. They may be nice but nice people can still be horse thieves.

8. Enter the composite writing sample into the RAFT template or display it on the chalkboard or whiteboard.

9. Have students review the sample to make sure it has covered all elements of RAFT(s). Remind students that the length of the piece doesn't matter as long as it uses all the required elements.

10. Assign the independent writing activity.

Reference

Daggett, W. *The Daggett System for Effective Instruction.* Rexford, NY: International Center for Leadership in Education, 2011.

For the Student

Independent Writing Activity

Follow these directions to write a RAFT assignment. Develop your writing appropriately by planning, revising, and editing.

1. Assign each group one of the RAFT rows in the completed chart on the next page. Allow each group to also choose, by themselves, one of the RAFT rows that they will work on next.

2. Students can also create their own RAFT assignment chart using the following blank template. Have them study the completed RAFT chart that follows to guide their choices. They would then use their own RAFT assignment to complete the writing activity.

3. Ask students to brainstorm possible approaches to each of the elements in the RAFT they were assigned. Students should suggest various approaches and ideas they would have for the role they're playing, the make-up of the audience, the aspects of the format, and the coverage of the topic.

4. Students should work in groups or alone if they wish to write an assignment, using the RAFT Composition Page found at the end of the assignment. They should be able to identify each element in their work and defend their completion of the assignment.

RAFT Assignment

Unit/Theme:		Language/Level:	
Role	Audience	Format	Topic

Sample RAFT Chart

RAFT Assignment

Unit/Theme:		Language/Level:	
Role	**Audience**	**Format**	**Topic**
George Washington	King of England	Gossip column	His public image in America
Artist	U.S. Supreme Court	Thank-you note	How she can paint without fear of repression
Cook	Vegetables	Recipe	How I will make you delicious
Adventurer	Advertisers	Web page	My trip to Saturn
Sperm whale	Television viewers	Travel guide	The amazing places I've visited
Comma	Readers everywhere	Letter to the editor	Why my work is unappreciated
Prison guard	Her children	Poem	What I have learned about prisoners
Dinosaur	Alligators	Diary	Things to avoid in the future
Reporter	Lewis and Clark expedition	Job description	What it takes to explore complete wilderness

RAFT Assignment (Continued)

Role	Audience	Format	Topic
A pizza	Neanderthal cave dwellers	Postcard	Greetings from the future of good eating
Repeating decimal	Set of rational numbers	Persuasive essay	Why you deserve to be part of that set
Any children's book characters	You, the reader	Minutes of a meeting	Why we decided you should be in our book
Rebel	A Chinese dynasty	Television sitcom script	Why your days are over
Water droplet	The clouds	News report	Water takes many forms
Inventor	The characters in *Titanic*	Advertisement	Why they will be saved from a shipwreck

_____

_____

_____

_____

_____

_____

_____

_____

_____

_____

RAFT Composition Page

Role of Writer:	Format:
Audience:	Topic:

_____
_____
_____
_____
_____
_____
_____
_____
_____
_____
_____
_____
_____
_____
_____
_____
_____
_____
_____
_____

◰ Scaffolding Note-taking

For the Teacher

Defining the Strategy

The only thing more challenging than taking notes for an analytical academic research paper is being unable to find some great idea you read in the middle of all that research. It's happened to every student at some point in the writing process. Either you can't find what you wrote down somewhere or you can't quite remember the gist of an idea but suddenly, it's the linchpin of the point you are trying to make. To avoid this nightmare, impose discipline on the note-taking process through the use of scaffolding.

Instructional scaffolding is an educational method you can use to organize and support your research process. Just as a set of scaffolding helps to build and support a building, a rigid framework of note-taking will help prepare and temporarily keep your research in place until it is strong enough on its own. Then, your scaffolding can be removed and your research can be turned into a term paper. Scaffolding adds context, motivation, and structure. Graphic organizers and flexible formats for your notes enable you to keep them accessible and most importantly, to avoid misplacing that crucial fact or quote when you need it most. Note-taking uses paraphrasing to determine the central ideas or themes of a text and analyze their development. Note-taking also helps you rethink the key supporting details and ideas while avoiding plagiarism or the overreliance on any one source. Note-taking also follows a standard format for citation. Finally, note-taking draws evidence from literary or informational texts to support analysis, reflection, and research.

In Quadrant D of the DSEI, the emphasis is on high rigor and high relevance. Students who employ the scaffolding note-taking technique are engaged in a student-generated activity that requires them to create note structures in an original way. They have to design a system that best suits the type of research they are conducting and best matches the paper they wish to write. In the process, they will become the recipients and judges of their own work as their notes will be tested through the process of writing an analytical academic research paper.

Applying the Strategy

Scaffolding note-taking is an effective strategy in most content areas and in middle and secondary programs.

Middle School

- Science
  - taking notes for labs that investigate physical phenomena
  - scaffolding the processes of the greenhouse effect
  - breaking down the stages of weather formation
- Social Studies
  - taking notes for a research paper on causes of westward migration
  - researching entries for a timeline
- Math
  - copying down steps to solve an algebraic equation
  - researching the lives of famous mathematicians and their breakthrough theories

- ELA
  - categorizing lecture notes during a group discussion about a literary work
  - researching a term paper about a character or a theme

Secondary School

- Science
  - defining the interactions of the parts of a cell
  - describing life processes in a biome
  - researching the forces at work during plate tectonics
- Social Studies
  - determining the political trends that swept Europe after World War I
  - researching philosophies and theologies in the history of religion
  - general research papers
- Math
  - recording steps in a geometric proof
  - breaking down the steps of a word problem
- ELA
  - citing passages in novels or longer works and matching them to aspects of a literary theory
  - scaffolding a term paper's research and determining if you've proven your opinion

Common Core State Standards

College and Career Readiness Anchor Standards for Writing

Text Types and Purposes

1. Write arguments to support claims in an analysis of substantive topics or texts, using valid reasoning and relevant and sufficient evidence.

2. Write informative/explanatory texts to examine and convey complex ideas and information clearly and accurately through the effective selection, organization, and analysis of content.

3. Write narratives to develop real or imagined experiences or events using effective technique, well-chosen details, and well-structured event sequences.

Production and Distribution of Writing

4. Produce clear and coherent writing in which the development, organization, and style are appropriate to task, purpose, and audience.

5. Develop and strengthen writing as needed by planning, revising, editing, rewriting, or trying a new approach.

Research to Build and Present Knowledge

7. Conduct short as well as more sustained research projects based on focused questions, demonstrating understanding of the subject under investigation.

8. Gather relevant information from multiple print and digital sources, assess the credibility and accuracy of each source, and integrate the information while avoiding plagiarism.

9. Draw evidence from literary or informational texts to support analysis, reflection, and research.

Teaching the Strategy

1. Introduce the strategy by explaining that scaffolding note-taking involves following a few established rules throughout the research process and sticking with them:

    -   **Use a variety of notes to match the research.** Some writers favor note cards that they can spread out on a table and switch around to reorganize at will; others like to put blocks of ideas in stacked charts on a yellow legal pad, and some writers like to create webs all over a page that can be linked to show connections. And many writers use all three types of organizers and often adapt them to computer or iPad applications as well.

    -   **Match your topic to your research or your research to your topic.** You may start with a strong topic, theme, or claim but as you conduct your research you may discover it needs to be tweaked or even reconsidered. Your research may also have to be changed to better match your topic. A strong organizational scaffold will help you match both research and topic.

    -   **Use paraphrasing and shorthanded notes.** Don't try to write everything down. It will not only slow you down but confuse your voice. Use a method of recording significant details and a means to retrieve them whenever you need them during your writing. Scaffolding will give you these capabilities.

    -   **Scaffolded notes act as an outline.** Order in your research translates to an ordered paper. If you take the time to record your research in an ordered form, the ideas and interconnections between parts of your research will lead you to a mode of presentation that replicates process of research in the final paper's structure.

    -   **Don't try to use all your research.** You will want to have more research than you might ever need. This way, you can comprehensively cover the topic and pick the most suitable items to make your point. You find those items by narrowing your sources to those on which you will concentrate the most.

- **Write it down if it catches your eye.** Don't judge your research. If something you come across interests you, jot it down or at least note where to find it again in case you need it. You can't be certain about what you will need until you're writing and you don't want to have to stop, at that point, in order to search for some tidbit that only would have taken a moment to record.

- **Leave plenty of space in your notes for other notes.** You will want to add comments or highlights to help guide you when using your notes during the writing. You may also come across other related information that you will want to add.

2. There are three different templates to assist writers in taking various types of notes, especially for independent research. The first one is for Scaffolding Note-taking. It can be recorded on a large file card or a regular sheet of paper.

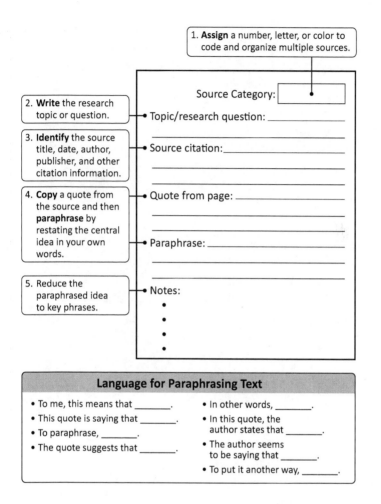

1. **Assign** a number, letter, or color to code and organize multiple sources.

2. **Write** the research topic or question.

3. **Identify** the source title, date, author, publisher, and other citation information.

4. **Copy** a quote from the source and then **paraphrase** by restating the central idea in your own words.

5. Reduce the paraphrased idea to key phrases.

Source Category: [ ]

Topic/research question: _____

Source citation:_____

Quote from page: _____

Paraphrase: _____

Notes:
-
-
-
-

Language for Paraphrasing Text

- To me, this means that _____.
- This quote is saying that _____.
- To paraphrase, _____.
- The quote suggests that _____.

- In other words, _____.
- In this quote, the author states that _____.
- The author seems to be saying that _____.
- To put it another way, _____.

3. The key to this method is proper paraphrasing. Remember that a paraphrase requires that you restate someone else's words and ideas in your own words. A good paraphrase keeps all the meaning but doesn't use a quote and can help you avoid plagiarism. Use the paraphrasing starters in the box shown here. In order to use these notes effectively, writers need to write down a few key phrases and ideas below the paraphrase that will enable them to quickly locate quotes or paraphrases. Consult the paraphrasing

strategy for further details that will show you how to use para-phrasing and scaffolding note-taking together.

4. Another layout for note-taking uses two columns and bullets or outline form. This layout works well for research and citations, and for taking notes on a chapter reading, a teacher lecture, or a video. The topics in the left-hand column allow you to quickly find your notes. If necessary, writers can add citation information and any coding to the top of the page.

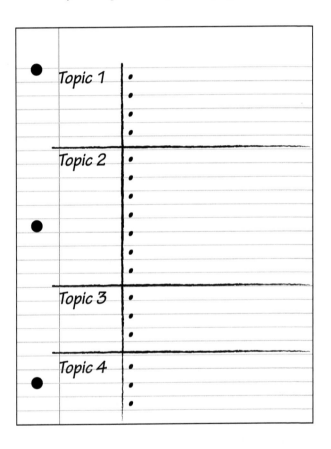

```
┌─────────────────────────────────────────────────┐
│                                                   │
│   ● Keywords: │ Notes:                            │
│   ─────────────────────────────────────────────  │
│        Topic 1 │ I.                               │
│                │   A.                             │
│                │   B.                             │
│                │   C.                             │
│                │                                  │
│        Topic 2 │ II.                              │
│   ●            │   A.                             │
│                │   B.                             │
│                │   C.                             │
│                │                                  │
│        Topic 3 │ III.                             │
│                │   A.                             │
│                │   B.                             │
│   ─────────────────────────────────────────────  │
│                                                   │
│     Summary:                                      │
│   ●                                               │
│                                                   │
└─────────────────────────────────────────────────┘
```

A web format like the following examples allows you to link related ideas around central themes. Citation information and paraphrases can be entered in each box and the layout can easily be adapted to any research, if necessary. Use this format for topics that are less focused on priority order or a sequence of events or steps. These formats allow writers to jot notes about a central theme or linked ideas.

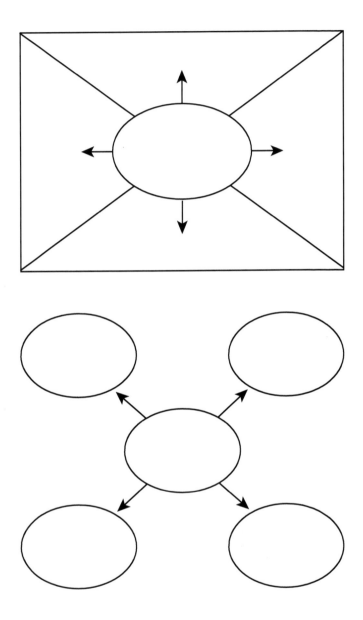

Directed Writing Activity

1. On a chalkboard, whiteboard, or overhead, display the following paragraph and explain that you are going to demonstrate how to create a scaffolded note.

Voyages and Travels: Ancient and Modern. The Harvard Classics. 1909–14. The Discovery of Guiana; Paras. 1–49: Sir Walter Raleigh. New York, P.F. Collier & Son Company

ON 12 Thursday, the sixth of February, in the year 1595, we departed England, and the Sunday following had sight of the north cape of Spain . . . We arrived at Trinidad the 22. of March, casting anchor at Point Curiapan, This island of Trinidad hath the form of a sheephook, and is but narrow; the north part is very mountainous; the soil is very excellent, and will bear sugar, ginger, or any other commodity that the Indies yield. It hath store of deer, wild porks, fruit, fish, and fowl; it hath also for bread sufficient maize, cassavi, and of those roots and fruits which are common everywhere in the West Indies. It hath divers beasts which the Indies have not; the Spaniards confessed that they found grains of gold in some of the rivers; but they having a purpose to enter Guiana, the magazine of all rich metals, cared not to spend time in the search thereof any further.

---

2. Display the Scaffolding Note-taking master.

3. Ask students to brainstorm possible numbering, lettering, or color codes that could be used in the upper right hand corner. For this example, use "Blue A1." The Blue can stand for historical accounts of the island of Trinidad, while Red could stand for current accounts, and Green can stand for statistical data. The

lettering can mark different authors and the numbering can indicate the pages on this particular author and work.

4. Discuss a possible topic/research question and then record it on the form. For example: *The island nation of Trinidad/Tobago is a "rainbow," a model of harmony among its different ethnic groups, cultures, and profitable industries.*

5. Enter the source citation: (Title) "Voyages and Travels: Ancient and Modern, The Harvard Classics (Date) 1909–14; (Author) Sir Walter Raleigh; (publisher) New York, P.F. Collier & Son Company; The Discovery of Guiana; Paras. 1–49

6. Copy a quote and give it a page number (page 1): "It hath divers beasts which the Indies have not; the Spaniards confessed that they found grains of gold in some of the rivers; but they having a purpose to enter Guiana, the magazine of all rich metals, cared not to spend time in the search thereof any further."

7. Paraphrase the quote: *Trinidad has a variety of animals that most of the islands in the West Indies do not have but it has little gold in its rivers, however the Spaniards didn't really search for it because they found plenty of gold in nearby Guiana.*

8. Notes:

   • 1595 Raleigh: deer, wild, pig, fish, fowl, fruit, good soil

   • Spanish: some gold in rivers

   • other metals in Guiana nearby

9. Discuss how another quote from the same source would be recorded on another form with a new page number. A new source would get another form with different coding.

10. Assign the independent writing activity. Students' note-taking from this source will vary. Students should select quotes that properly match a topic they create. They should also make up an organizing system for the Source Category. From the source provided or other research materials, they should produce three separate pages of notes, for three separate quotes. The notes taken should match the original source and be accurate.

Reference

Jones, R. *Using Rigor and Relevance to Create Effective Instruction*. Rexford, NY: International Center for Leadership in Education, 2012.

Independent Writing Activity

Follow these directions to do your own scaffolding note-taking. Use the template or design one of your own. As you did in the Direct Writing Activity, gather the relevant information from the informational text provided to support analysis, reflection, and research. Integrate the information while avoiding plagiarism.

1. Use the paragraphs below as a source for research. Make up your own topic and select quotes you would need for your notes. Make up your own organizing system for the Source Category.

2. Produce three separate pages of notes, for three separate quotes. You could also use other research materials if they are available and practice taking notes from them.

3. Share notes with a partner. Then, critique each other's work. Be sure to compare the notes to the original source and make sure the information is accurate.

From *Robert's Rules of Order; Revised for Deliberative Assemblies*; 4. Motions and Resolutions. Henry M. Robert (1837–1923). Chicago: Scott, Foresman, 1915

A motion is a proposal that the assembly take certain action, or that it express itself as holding certain views. It is made by a member's obtaining the floor as already described and saying, "I move that" (which is equivalent to saying, "I propose that"), and then stating the action he proposes to have taken. Thus a member "moves" (proposes) that a resolution be adopted, or amended, or referred to a committee, or that a vote of thanks be extended, etc.; or "That it is the sense of this meeting (or assembly) that industrial training," etc. Every resolution should be in writing, and the presiding officer has a right to require any main motion, amendment, or instructions to a committee to be in writing. When a main motion is of such importance or length as to be in writing it is usually written in the form of a resolution; that is, beginning with the words, "Resolved, That," the word "Resolved" being underscored (printed in italics) and followed by a comma, and the word "That" beginning with a capital "T." If the word "Resolved" were replaced by the words "I move," the resolution would become a motion. A resolution is always a main motion. In some sections of the country the word "resolve" is frequently used instead of "resolution." In assemblies with paid employees, instructions given to employees are called "orders" instead of "resolutions," and the enacting word, "Ordered" is used instead of "Resolved."

As a general rule no member can make two motions at a time except by general consent. But he may combine the motion to suspend the rules with the motion for whose adoption it was made; and the motion to reconsider a resolution and its amendments; and a member may offer a resolution and at the same time move to make it a special order for a specified time.

As a general rule, with the exceptions given below, every motion should be seconded. This is to prevent time being consumed in considering a question that only one person favors, and consequently little attention is paid to it in routine motions. Where the chair is certain the motion meets with general favor, and yet members are slow about seconding it, he may proceed without waiting for a second. Yet, any one may make a point of order that the motion has not been seconded, and then the chair is obliged to proceed formally and call for a second. The better way when a motion is not at once seconded, is for the chair to ask, "Is the motion seconded?" A motion is seconded by a member's saying, "I second the motion," or "I second it," which he does without obtaining the floor, and in small assemblies without rising.

"The question is on the adoption of the resolution [which the chair reads]; those in favor of the resolution say aye; those opposed say no. The ayes have it, and the resolution is adopted;" or, "The noes have it, and the resolution is lost."

Scaffolding Note-taking Master

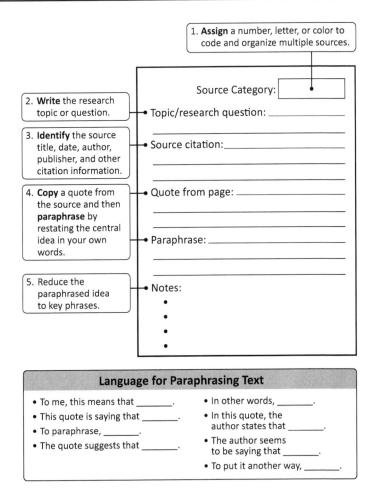

1. **Assign** a number, letter, or color to code and organize multiple sources.

2. **Write** the research topic or question.

3. **Identify** the source title, date, author, publisher, and other citation information.

4. **Copy** a quote from the source and then **paraphrase** by restating the central idea in your own words.

5. Reduce the paraphrased idea to key phrases.

Source Category:

Topic/research question: _____

Source citation: _____

Quote from page: _____

Paraphrase: _____

Notes:
-
-
-
-

Language for Paraphrasing Text

- To me, this means that _____.
- This quote is saying that _____.
- To paraphrase, _____.
- The quote suggests that _____.

- In other words, _____.
- In this quote, the author states that _____.
- The author seems to be saying that _____.
- To put it another way, _____.

Semantic Feature Analysis Chart

For the Teacher

Defining the Strategy

Teachers and students have used a semantic feature analysis chart primarily as a tool to increase vocabulary acquisition, content retention, and reading comprehension through the application of prior knowledge and categorizing. However, semantic feature analysis can also assist students with their writing. After students have researched a topic, they often fail to organize and relate connected concepts. With the skill of semantic feature analysis they can better plan, conceptualize, and outline how they will advance a claim in argument writing, explain a concept in informational/explanatory writing, or tell an effective story in narrative writing. Using a semantic feature analysis chart will help students both conjoin their interconnected ideas and make distinctions among them. This chart is particularly effective for technical reports where much of the information must be put into a chart or graph and the rest of the writing involves bulleted points explaining the chart.

Semantic feature analysis will allow students to develop and strengthen writing as needed by planning, revising, editing, rewriting, or trying a new approach. Writers get a fresh take on familiar material, too, by breaking it down and developing it in a manner appropriate to task, purpose, and audience. Defining similarities and differences in their research results will help students see this material with a redefined perspective.

The Application Model found in the Rigor/Relevance Framework offers five levels on a continuum that describes Application of Knowledge. We also can see this continuum at work in a semantic feature analysis chart. Students begin with knowledge in one discipline or a set of prior knowledge parameters and then apply this knowledge across other disciplines or areas of expertise. As students compare and contrast different yet related sets of information they are applying to real-world predictable situations the evidence and information from multiple print and digital resources that they have researched along with their prior knowledge. As they use the observations that the chart offers them, they are applying what they have acquired to regenerated uses and real-world unpredictable situations.

Applying the Strategy

A Semantic Feature Analysis Chart is an effective writing strategy in most content areas and in middle and secondary programs.

Middle School
- Science
  - defining characteristics in animal and plant classifications
  - comparing the planets and other heavenly bodies
  - classifying properties of rocks and elements
- Social Studies
  - comparing historical periods and personalities
  - analyzing political and economic systems
- Math
  - comparing similarities in sets
  - defining differences in mathematical properties

- ELA
  - defining elements of genres
  - comparing themes, characters, and grammatical functions of words

Secondary School

- Science
  - comparing chemicals in the periodic table of elements
  - organizing biological necessities of different environments
  - comparing properties of wave behavior and optical effects
- Social Studies
  - aligning trends and their origins in earlier eras
  - similarities of economic systems
  - breaking down the consequences of economic events
- Math
  - comparing geometrical shapes and their properties
  - analyzing mathematical solutions and methods
  - determining commonality in computer programming
- ELA
  - comparing aspects of genres
  - analyzing motivations of characters and authors
  - classifying characteristics of poetry
  - determining elements of authors' styles

Common Core State Standards

College and Career Readiness Anchor Standards for Writing

Text Types and Purposes

1. Write arguments to support claims in an analysis of substantive topics or texts, using valid reasoning and relevant and sufficient evidence.

2. Write informative/explanatory texts to examine and convey complex ideas and information clearly and accurately through the effective selection, organization, and analysis of content.

3. Write narratives to develop real or imagined experiences or events using effective technique, well-chosen details, and well-structured event sequences.

Production and Distribution of Writing

4. Produce clear and coherent writing in which the development, organization, and style are appropriate to task, purpose, and audience.

5. Develop and strengthen writing as needed by planning, revising, editing, rewriting, or trying a new approach.

Research to Build and Present Knowledge

6. Conduct short as well as more sustained research projects based on focused questions, demonstrating understanding of the subject under investigation.

7. Conduct short as well as more sustained research projects based on focused questions, demonstrating understanding of the subject under investigation.

8. Gather relevant information from multiple print and digital sources, assess the credibility and accuracy of each source, and integrate the information while avoiding plagiarism.

Teaching the Strategy

Introduce the strategy by explaining that using the semantic feature analysis chart will assist both reading and writing in the following ways:

- **Noting similarities and differences.** Many different types of writing require writers to distinguish one idea from another and to make distinctions based on details. Semantic analysis helps writers recognize similarities and differences among a group of events, people, objects, or concepts they are trying to analyze.

- **Organizing research.** Often writers will acquire sets of seemingly disparate information, but a semantic feature analysis will allow them to see how these can be related. Writers can also use the chart to make predictions, visualize connections, and master larger concepts.

- **Relating vocabulary to key features.** By concentrating on specific vocabulary, writers expand and better understand the meanings that allow them to group words into logical categories.

- **Using semantic analysis for writing.** Once they have constructed a semantic analysis chart, writers can use the information obtained to create an original work. In a technical report, the chart itself may be the primary piece of writing created.

Words and ideas can be analyzed individually and semantically by developing word associations among research terms. Doing so will also help students extend their content knowledge. There are two similar approaches in this analysis; the first is the precursor to the second.

- **Word Map.** This graphic organizer can serve as a warm-up for each word. Students can take a word like *mountain,* which is part of a larger category, and associate it with other words with related meanings. Have students note how the term *mountain* is expanded into its class (*biome*), into parts of a mountain (*peak, cliff, foothills, ridge, range*), and examples (*Rocky Mountains, the Alps*). This same process can be used for almost any research item.

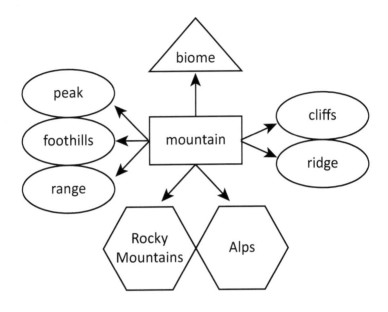

- **Semantic Analysis Chart Matrix.** In the second approach, concepts or terms are listed along the left side of a chart and then compared to each other by their features or characteristics listed along the top of a chart. A plus sign (+) means it has this characteristic. A minus sign (–) means it does not. If an item can go either way, a plus/minus sign is entered.

Concept/Term	Characteristics			
States	On ocean	Mountains	Heavily populated	Generally warm
Oregon	+	+	–	+/–
Florida	+	–	+	+
North Dakota	–	+/–	–	–

An analysis of this chart could conclude a few things. If you wanted to write about heavily populated states in warm climates near the ocean, Florida would be a good place to start. If you were considering areas of the country where someone seeking low population density didn't care about a warm climate and taking surfing lessons, then North Dakota would be a good place to start.

Directed Writing Activity

1. This activity will require students to produce clear and coherent writing in which development, organization, and style are appropriate to task and purpose. Students can create a matrix as a whole class, in small groups, or individually. Monitoring the progress of the chart's creation will reveal the depth of student knowledge about the subject. Students can be redirected to research more details about the topic or about individual characteristics. Students can create a word map to explore any individual word or term they wish to consider. This will allow them to explore all aspects of a term.

2. Display the blank semantic feature analysis charts shown below. Students can adjust either the number of columns or rows to match what they're analyzing.

3. Ask students to identify a topic to be analyzed. As an example, students might wish to write a fairy tale narrative but need to discover the elements commonly included in fairy tales.

4. Down the left hand side of the chart they would list different fairy tales that they have read and wish to analyze. Students can add to the ones shown.

5. Across the top of the chart, they would list as many characteristics or features of fairytales as they know. Keep in mind that these don't need to be common to all or even a majority of fairy tales, just a feature found in one example that they found in their research. Again, students can add other features.

6. Have students debate, if necessary, the inclusion of a given feature or characteristic. Students should also note an example or examples of this feature. Review, if necessary, the basic plots of classic fairy tales.

7. After students complete the chart, have them analyze the results. Ask students to look for trends and compare the stories in terms of the elements they share or lack. Encourage students to look for relationships and connections.

8. As a composition expansion of the chart, now ask students to consider the type of fairy tale they would like to write on their own. Have them consider the characteristics in the chart and formulate a story based on these appearing or not appearing in their stories. For example, almost every story has magic and a test that the hero has to pass. Their stories could feature these elements or avoid them for special effect.

9. Students should go over their story and analyze its plot using the chart. They could also add other categories and characteristics.

10. Assign the independent writing activity.

Sample Semantic Feature Analysis Chart

Concept/Term	Characteristics							
Characters	Foolish behavior	Hero must pass test	Magic	Evil siblings	Witch	Monster	Strange humans	Precautionary tale
Snow White	+	+	+	–	+	–	+	–
Sleeping Beauty	–	+	+	–	+	–	–	–
Rumpelstiltskin	+	+	+	–	–	–	+	+
Beauty and the Beast	–	+	+	+	–	+	–	–
Jack and the Beanstalk	+	+	+	–	–	+	–	+
Pied Piper	+	+/–	+	–	–	–	+	+/–

Reference

Jones, R. *Rigor and Relevance Handbook*. Rexford, NY: International Center for Leadership in Education, 2010.

For the Student

Independent Writing Activity

Follow these directions to create a semantic feature analysis chart. Develop your writing appropriately by planning, revising, and editing.

1. Select a category of your own choosing or use the suggestions listed below. Gather as many characteristics and features as you can brainstorm. Use research materials if available or use prior knowledge.

    *   presidents of the United States

    *   characters or plot elements from a novel or a series of novels

    *   relatives from your family

    *   countries around the world

    *   animals in the zoo

    *   which car to purchase

    *   which college to choose

2. Keep in mind that you will use the chart to write a short paragraph or two about your category and use the chart to fill out all the details you want to include.

3. Complete your own semantic feature analysis chart. Allow as many columns or rows as necessary to accommodate what you are analyzing.

4. Carefully analyze the chart you created and let it guide you for making connections and including details.

5. Write an argument with a claim, an expository essay to inform or explain, or a narrative that tells a story using the observations you have made with your semantic feature analysis chart.

Semantic Feature Analysis Chart

Characteristics				
Concept/Term				

Story Pyramid

For the Teacher

Defining the Strategy

The Story Pyramid is a visual tool that teachers sometimes use to aid or assess reading comprehension, but it also can be used to help students focus their thoughts as they prepare to write narratives. It encourages writers to focus on the key elements of the narrative they are considering, thus helping them develop and strengthen writing by spending more time planning. As a prewriting graphic organizer, the Story Pyramid encourages the strategic use of visual displays of data to express information that students will flesh out as they draft their writing. It provides help with an early step in the writing process, and helps ensure that students produce clear and coherent writing in which the development, organization, and style are appropriate to the task, purpose, and audience.

When students work with a Story Pyramid, they demonstrate Quadrant B thinking in the Rigor/Relevance Framework, since it helps them apply their understanding of how narratives work to the creation of an original narrative. The complexity required to summarize ideas and create a narrative also requires Quadrant D thinking. A Story Pyramid may appear simple, but it fits the call of the DSEI for a culture of high expectations: It encourages making connections across the curriculum and requires students to distill and express their thoughts in a "shorthand" that will prompt further thought.

Applying the Strategy

The word *story* suggests that a Story Pyramid is used for planning works of fiction. Indeed, the strategy is used most often for fiction writing, but its value extends to *any* kind of writing that requires a sequential structure. Thus, a Story Pyramid can help students write narratives to develop real or imagined experiences or events, but it also can help students write informative/explanatory texts in many areas of the curriculum. Used creatively, it even can be extended to some kinds of persuasive/argument writing.

Middle School

- **Reading/ELA**
  - creating an original short story (any genre), anecdote, or skit (all forms of narrative writing)
  - retelling a grade-appropriate narrative that the class has read together or the student has read independently
- **Social Studies**
  - creating a short historical fiction narrative based on a person or event discussed in class
  - preparing an informative biographical presentation of a historical figure whom students admire
- **Science**
  - explaining a developmental process (for example, the formation and effects of a hurricane) in narrative form
- **Health**
  - creating an original narrative (such as a short story) that focuses on the application of a health issue in everyday life (for example, receiving a medical treatment)
  - presenting an anecdote about a behavioral change (for example, adopting an exercise routine)

- **The Arts**
  - writing a skit that imagines the creation of a famous work of art
  - preparing a plot synopsis as part of a movie proposal (any genre, but a form of argument writing)

Secondary School

- **Reading/ELA**
  - creating a story (any genre) told over several chapters, an autobiographical account, or a short play
  - as part of a literary analysis, retelling the plot of a classic work of American or British literature
- **Social Studies**
  - creating a short story with a setting that accurately describes life in another culture
  - presenting an extended first-person narrative that relates historically correct information about an important event
- **Science**
  - tracing milestones in the development of scientific theories
  - creating a short play about an important scientific discovery or invention
- **Health**
  - creating a short play that focuses on conflict resolution
  - presenting an autobiographical sketch that explains nutrition in a humorous way
- **The Arts**
  - presenting an informative biography about a famous artist or musician
  - creating a synopsis as part of a review (a form of argument writing) of a movie or a stage play

Common Core State Standards

College and Career Readiness Anchor Standards for Writing

Text Types and Purposes

2. Write informative/explanatory texts to examine and convey complex ideas and information clearly and accurately through the effective selection, organization, and analysis of content.

3. Write narratives to develop real or imagined experiences or events using elective technique, well-chosen details, and well-structured event sequences.

Production and Distribution of Writing

4. Produce clear and coherent writing in which the development, organization, and style are appropriate to task, purpose, and audience.

5. Develop and strengthen writing as needed by planning, revising, editing, rewriting, or trying a new approach.

Range of Writing

10. Write routinely over extended time frames (time for research, reflection, and revision) and shorter time frames (a single sitting or a day or two) for a range of tasks, purposes, and audiences.

College and Career Readiness Anchor Standards for Speaking and Listening

Presentation of Knowledge and Ideas

5. Make strategic use of digital media and visual displays of data to express information and enhance understanding of presentations.

Teaching the Strategy

Introduce the strategy by noting that much of our communication could be classified as "storytelling." For example, forms of storytelling can include summarizing the plot of a TV show that we watched, relating a humorous personal experience, or explaining the key moments in a historical event or movement. Indeed, storytelling seems to be a fundamental part of the human experience, regardless of culture or time period. Sometimes the story details are facts, and sometimes they are products of the imagination. In either case, however, they make a point and are presented in a sequence that has a clear beginning, middle, and end.

Point out that when we want to write an effective story (whether fiction or nonfiction), it is important for us to plan. It is especially important to make decisions, ahead of time, about the focus of the narrative (a main character, in fiction; a clear topic, in nonfiction), its key events, and its "point" (its main idea, theme, or lesson, whether stated or implied).

For younger students, or for students who are new to this kind of planning, model a simple five-level Story Pyramid, based on the movie *Star Wars: A New Hope*. Give these instructions, followed by the graphic organizer.

1. In one word, name the main character.
2. In two words, describe the main character.
3. In three words, describe the setting.
4. In four words, name an early event.
5. In five words, name the last event.

1. Luke

2. Seeks adventure

3. Some distant galaxy

4. Finds Princess Leia's message

5. Destroys Darth Vader's Death Star

As you discuss the model, point out the kinds of information that it records. Emphasize that completing a Story Pyramid is not merely a matter of filling in blanks; it requires the user to have some thoughts in mind and then to state those thoughts very succinctly. If students comment that there is much more to the movie's plot than this, agree but explain that a Story Pyramid is meant to capture just enough key information to remind users of the essence of the story. This fact applies both to recalling a narrative that students have read or viewed and also to creating an original narrative.

Next, explain that a typical Story Pyramid includes more details and thus contains more levels. An eight-level Story Pyramid is quite common. The following example illustrates a Story Pyramid that might capture the essence of *The Adventures of Tom Sawyer*.

1. In one word, name the main character.
2. In two words, describe the main character.
3. In three words, describe the setting.
4. In four words, name a problem that the main character faces.
5. In five words, name an important story event.
6. In six words, name a second important story event.
7. In seven words, name the event that is the climax of the story.
8. In eight words, name the solution to the character's problem.

(In some cases, Steps 7 and 8 can be combined, leaving room for a step in which students describe the "lesson" of the story, or a Step 9 can be added to accomplish the same goal.)

1. Tom

2. Mischievous bold

3. St. Petersburg Missouri 1840s

4. Being "responsible" not "'childish"

5. Witness Injun Joe commit murder

6. Fearfully testifies against Joe in court

7. Encounters Joe while lost in McDougal's Cave

8. Proves responsibility by saving himself and Becky Thatcher

The preceding example was used for a work of fiction, but a similar Story Pyramid could help students plan their own writing of a biography or autobiography.

Some adaptation will be needed to use a Story Pyramid with nonfiction topics that outline a process. The following model, which captures key elements in the "narrative" of human respiration, can serve for any number of such processes, with the number of steps adjusted as needed.

1. In one word, name the process.
2. In two words, describe the process.
3. In three words, describe the importance of the process.
4. In four words, explain the first step in the process.
5. In five words, explain the second step in the process.
6. In six words, explain the third step in the process.
7. In seven words, explain the fourth step in the process.
8. In eight words, explain the fifth step in the process.
9. In nine words, explain the final step in the process.

1. Respiration

2. Automatic complex

3. Human survival necessity

4. Air enters through inhalation

5. Travels down trachea to bronchi

6. Moves into bronchioles and expanding alveoli

7. Oxygen in air-filled alveoli passes into capillaries

8. Carbon dioxide in capillaries passes into alveoli air

9. After exchange of gases carbon dioxide released through inhalation

Directed Writing Activity

1. Brainstorm with students to develop original story ideas. You may wish to use a variety of sentence frames, such as the following, to stir students' creativity:

   - The moment I walked into (my room, the gym, my new homeroom), I knew that _____.

   - The (general, guide, captain) thought, "The only way that we can survive is to _____."

   - Suddenly, they saw a(n) _____ (in the sky, on the horizon, under a tree).

   - When it was all over, I exclaimed, "No one will ever believe that we _____!"

Take a class vote to choose the idea that students will develop.

2. Copy and distribute the form for an Eight-Level Story Pyramid (Fiction or Nonfiction Narrative). Depending upon the amount of time you give this activity, either have students complete it in class or do it as homework; just be aware that students will need a little time to choose the best way to summarize their ideas at each level and that students will not all work at the same speed.

3. When students have completed their Story Pyramid, have them meet in small groups to share their ideas. Urge group members to respond positively to each other's story ideas and to discuss how various ideas could be developed further. Guide students to see that the same beginning idea can be developed in numerous ways. Have each group choose one Story Pyramid — either one that a group member has submitted or a new one that group members collaborate to create — to present to the entire class.

4. After discussing the groups' presentations, encourage students to review the Story Pyramid that they created before meeting with their group. Invite students to write a story, based on the graphic organizer, and to publish it in a format of their (or your) choosing.

References

Atwell, Nancie. *In the Middle: New Understandings About Writing, Reading, and Learning*. Portsmouth, NH: Boynton/Cook, Heinemann, 1998.

Carr, Eileen, Aldinger, Loviah, and Patberg, Judythe. *Teaching Comprehension: A Systematic and Practical Framework with Lessons and Strategies*. New York, NY: Scholastic/ThinkingWorks, 2004.

Ellery, Valerie. and Rosenboom, Jennifer L. *Sustaining Strategic Readers: Techniques for Supporting Content Literacy in Grades 6–12*. Newark, DE: International Reading Association, 2011.

Macon, James M., Bewell, Diane, and Vogt, MaryEllen. *Responses to Literature: Grades K–8*. Newark, DE: International Reading Association, 1991.

McAndrews, Stephanie L. *Diagnostic Literacy Assessments and Instructional Strategies: A Literacy Specialist's Resource*. Newark, DE: International Reading Association, 2008.

For the Student

Independent Writing Activity

Follow these directions to plan a piece of writing by using a Story Pyramid.

1. Choose a writing idea. Here are some suggestions, but you may create your own.

Fiction Narrative	Nonfiction Narrative	Nonfiction Process
• a short story about some teens who make an amazing discovery • a play about a person who must make a difficult decision	• an anecdote about yourself or a family member • a biography of an important person in history	• an explanation of how a nation gained its independence • an explanation of how a force of nature develops

2. Spend a few minutes thinking about your idea. Take notes so that you can remember some of the details that come to mind.

3. Decide which Story Pyramid form will work better for your idea.

   • If you choose an idea for a fiction or nonfiction narrative, use the Eight-Level Story Pyramid. Follow the directions to identify the main character, the setting, and key events in the narrative.

   • If you choose an idea for a nonfiction process, use the Nine-Level Story Pyramid. Follow the directions to identify the process, its importance, and its key steps. (If the process has fewer than six key steps, delete levels as needed.)

4. Share your Story Pyramid with a partner. Does it make sense to your partner? What questions does he or she have about your writing idea? Which of those questions will you address if you create a piece of writing that is based on your Story Pyramid?

5. If you wish, draft a piece of writing. Flesh out the information from your Story Pyramid by adding details and dialogue (if you are creating a story or play) and by creating an interesting beginning and ending. In addition, make sure that the events in the narrative or the steps in the process are clear, that they appear in the correct order, and that they are connected in a way that makes the writing "flow." Do these things again when you review your draft. At that time, also check your grammar, spelling, and punctuation. Finally, make a clean copy and share your writing with your audience.

Eight-Level Story Pyramid (Fiction or Nonfiction Narrative)

1. In one word, name the main character.
2. In two words, describe the main character.
3. In three words, describe the setting.
4. In four words, name a problem that the main character faces.
5. In five words, name an important story event.
6. In six words, name a second important story event.
7. In seven words, name the event that is the climax of the story.
8. In eight words, name the solution to the character's problem.

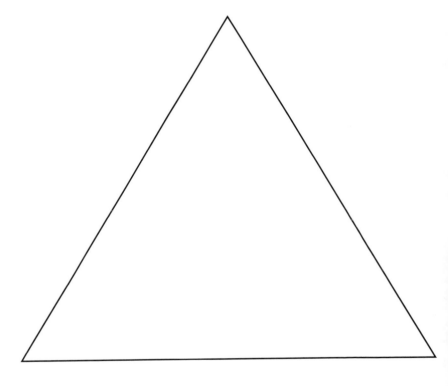

Nine-Level Story Pyramid (Nonfiction Process)

1. In one word, name the process.
2. In two words, describe the process.
3. In three words, describe the importance of the process.
4. In four words, explain the first step in the process.
5. In five words, explain the second step in the process.
6. In six words, explain the third step in the process.
7. In seven words, explain the fourth step in the process.
8. In eight words, explain the fifth step in the process.
9. In nine words, explain the final step in the process.

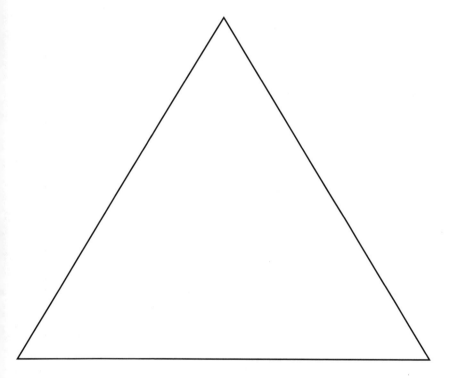

■ Take and Pass

Defining the Strategy

This strategy is a form of peer review or consultation. It can be used at different times in the writing process. Students work in a small group of four or five, commenting or providing responses to each other's work. It may also be used to gather information about a particular topic. For example, if students in a group of five each read a different article about the same topic, they can share this information using the Take and Pass strategy.

The Take and Pass strategy first asks students in a small group to arrange themselves in a circle. If the assignment is to write a response to literature, after writing their responses, each student will pass their response to the student on their right. Each student would then have the writing of one of their peers and could comment on the writing. Again, when they are finished, they pass the writing to their right. The process continues until the writing ends up back with the original author.

By using the Take and Pass strategy, students will have the opportunity to examine and convey complex ideas and information. The feedback they receive will help them to select, organize, and analyze the content of their writing effectively. In addition, they will have the opportunity to practice their peer-review skills by providing constructive criticism aimed at improving a classmate's writing.

This writing strategy requires learners to gather and store information, use knowledge to analyze and solve problems, evaluate problems and create solutions, and apply their knowledge to new situations. As such, the Take and Pass strategy fits in every Quadrant of the Rigor/Relevance Framework, depending on the writing task at hand.

Applying the Strategy

This strategy is appropriate to use for narrative writing, informative and explanatory writing, and argument writing tasks. The strategy supports standards 1 and 9 of the Common Core College and Career Anchor Standards for Writing. Standard 1 focuses on writing arguments using valid reasoning and sufficient evidence. The Take and Pass strategy provides a quick and easy way for writers to get feedback on whether their reasoning makes sense and whether they are using sufficient evidence to support it.

The focus of Anchor standard 9 is on drawing evidence from literary or informational texts to support analysis, reflection, and research. Again, the Take and Pass strategy can be used to assess whether the evidence a writer employs does, in fact, support their analysis, reflection, or research.

The Take and Pass strategy can be used across all content areas in middle and secondary programs.

Middle School

- Science
  - adding information to summaries of group experiments
- Social Studies
  - providing feedback on peer writing
  - completing historical timelines
  - writing about cause and effect

- Math
  - checking peer work and solutions
- ELA
  - organizing concepts, ideas, and information
  - using proper mechanics

Secondary School

- Science
  - writing group lab reports
- Social Studies
  - providing peer feedback on historical essays
  - deeply researching time periods and events
- Math
  - assessing peer solutions and explanations
- ELA
  - organizing concepts, ideas, and information
  - using proper mechanics

Common Core State Standards

College and Career Readiness Anchor Standards for Writing

Text Types and Purposes

1. Write arguments to support claims in an analysis of substantive topics or texts using valid reasoning and relevant and sufficient evidence.

2. Write informative/explanatory texts to examine and convey complex ideas and information clearly and accurately through the effective selection, organization, and analysis of content.

Production and Distribution of Writing

4. Produce clear and coherent writing in which the development, organization, and style are appropriate to task, purpose, and audience.

5. Develop and strengthen writing as needed by planning, revising, editing, rewriting, or trying a new approach.

Research to Build and Present Knowledge

7. Conduct short as well as more sustained research projects based on focused questions, demonstrating understanding of the subject under investigation.

8. Gather relevant information from multiple print and digital sources, assess the credibility and accuracy of each source, and integrate the information while avoiding plagiarism.

9. Draw evidence from literary or informational texts to support analysis, reflection, and research.

Range of Writing

10. Write routinely over extended time frames (time for research, reflection, and revision) and shorter time frames (a single sitting or a day or two) for a range of tasks, purposes, and audiences.

Teaching the Strategy

To introduce the strategy to students, present the saying "Two heads are better than one." Discuss the saying with students and explore how it is true pertaining to writing. Point out that novels are not published without being thoroughly edited by a person who did not write the book.

The purposes of the Take and Pass strategy include:

- **Providing feedback.** Depending on the writing task, the Take and Pass strategy provides an excellent way to give and receive peer feedback on a piece of writing. It also provides a writer with several peer suggestions in a short amount of time. Peer feedback from more than one peer is helpful in that different people may read the writing differently and have different ideas about how to improve it.

- **Gathering information.** The Take and Pass strategy can be used when first beginning a project to gather information. For example, if a new topic is being introduced in science, students in a group may each write one fact or characteristic they already know about the topic. Ideally, when their paper returns to them, students will gain new information about the topic.

- **Consolidating information.** The Take and Pass strategy can be used when there is a large piece of reading that can be broken down. Each student can be responsible for reading a portion of the text. Then they can use the Take and Pass strategy to share what they learned with others in the group.

Many different tools can be used for the Take and Pass strategy. For gathering information, a graphic organizer such as a concept map may be helpful. If the goal of a Take and Pass is to edit a peer's writing for mechanics, introduce editing marks. If the task is to assist in revision, students can complete writing frames like the one shown below and attach them to the writing.

One effective part of your (writing/project) was _____
_____
because _____
_____
One question I have is _____
_____
As you revise, be sure to _____
_____

The Take and Pass strategy really allows you to be creative. It can be used for any type of writing and the feedback can be structured in many ways. The types of information that can be gathered using this strategy are also limitless.

Directed Writing Activity

1. In this activity, students will use the Take and Pass strategy to gather information on a specific topic. Assign a topic with which they are familiar, but which they have not specifically studied in the last six months. Examples might include topics such as the solar system, the Declaration of Independence, or how to write a how-to paragraph.

2. Place students in small groups of four to five students. Give each student a copy of the concept map. Ask them to write the topic in the middle square and then list a fact or characteristic, or a piece of knowledge about the topic in one of the outer rectangles.

3. Have students pass their concept maps to the student on their right. Ask them to complete another outer rectangle of the concept map. Point out that they should read all of the information on the concept map first, and make every effort not to repeat the information.

4. Once the concept maps have moved all of the way around the circle of students, have groups use them to create a group concept map. They should make sure that all of the information they came up with is included.

5. Next, use the group concept maps to complete a class concept map on the board. Discuss how the Take and Pass strategy facilitated the exchange of a great deal of information in a short amount of time.

Sample Concept Map

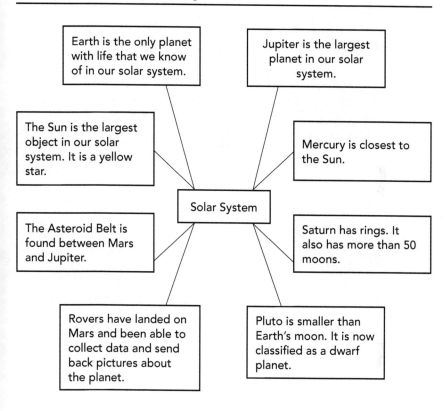

Earth is the only planet with life that we know of in our solar system.

Jupiter is the largest planet in our solar system.

The Sun is the largest object in our solar system. It is a yellow star.

Mercury is closest to the Sun.

Solar System

The Asteroid Belt is found between Mars and Jupiter.

Saturn has rings. It also has more than 50 moons.

Rovers have landed on Mars and been able to collect data and send back pictures about the planet.

Pluto is smaller than Earth's moon. It is now classified as a dwarf planet.

For the Student

Independent Writing Activity

Follow these directions to write a short argument. You will use the argument to practice the Take and Pass strategy with your classmates. While you should give consideration to your writing, giving and receiving feedback should be your main focus.

1. Write a short argument using this writing prompt:

   In most places, boys and girls compete on separate sports teams. What if a boy wanted to compete in a sport for which his school only has a girl's team? Or say, on the other hand, a girl wants to compete in a sport for which her school only has a boy's team. Should they be allowed to compete? How would it work? Support your opinion with strong reasons and evidence.

2. Staple two copies of the feedback form to your writing. When everyone in your group is ready, use the Take and Pass strategy to give each other feedback.

3. Once you have received feedback from your peers, use the feedback to revise and edit your writing.

Concept Map

Concept Map

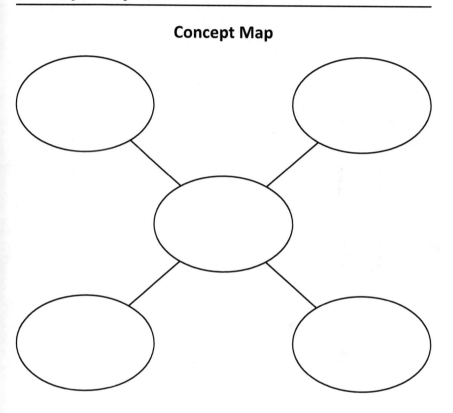

Peer Feedback

Responder: _____

A very effective argument in your writing is _____
_____
_____

because _____

One question I have is _____
_____

As you revise, I suggest _____
_____
_____

◲ Thesis Statement

For the Teacher

Defining the Strategy

Constructing a thesis statement from your research is a bit like describing a car from a walk through a junkyard. The writer has to assemble a clear unifying statement from a jumble of ideas. You may have started your research with a thesis or a claim to argue and then found all the support you need to begin writing, but you still have to craft an overall thesis, a sort of "super" topic sentence that will define the whole paper, as well as specific "lesser" topic sentences to define the main meaning of each subsequent paragraph.

A strong thesis statement is always a complete sentence that accomplishes two major tasks. The writer chooses a subject that's (1) limited enough to be dealt with in a short paper or a paragraph and (2) also expresses a precise opinion or controlling idea that states an intent or attitude towards the subject. Think of a thesis statement as an introduction in which the writer suggests a fascinating concept and then renders an attitude towards it. Writers need their topic conceptions to be precise and emphatic. These sentences tell readers what they should be concerned about and preview the information they are about to learn. Good writers challenge their readers and present thesis statements as sign posts, each with a carefully worded and restrictive focus that both generates and controls information. The writing that follows a thesis statement fills it out, explains it, or justifies its claims, opinions, narratives, or explanations. In short, it embodies the ideas set forth in the thesis statement and embraces them. If a strong thesis statement is developed, writing the rest of an essay or paper becomes much easier. Moreover, having a strong thesis statement in an introductory paragraph makes it easier for a writer to create strong topic sentences in the rest of the paragraphs to support the thesis statement.

Thesis statements are used in all types of analytical academic writing. They often form the claim of an argument while the rest of the paragraph uses valid reasoning and relevant and sufficient evidence to prove the claim. In informative/explanatory texts thesis statements are used to examine and convey complex ideas and information clearly and accurately through the effective selection, organization, and analysis of content. Within narratives, thesis statements develop real or imagined experiences or events using effective technique, well-chosen details, and well-structured event sequences. A thesis statement will also introduce a topic and organize complex ideas, concepts, and information so that each new element builds on that which precedes it to create a unified whole.

Within the skills matrix of the Rigor/Relevance Framework, the construction of an appropriate thesis statement requires students to use acquired knowledge from their research to complete a work. This task falls within Quadrant B and, as students write paragraphs or essays that flesh out the topic, they create unique solutions and take action, functioning therefore within Quadrants C and D.

Applying the Strategy

Writing thesis statements is an effective strategy in most content areas and in middle and secondary programs.

Middle School

- Science
  - organizing a science report
  - describing predicted behavior of moving objects
  - explaining the functions of simple machines

- Social Studies
  - analyzing historical documents
  - conceiving a report about changes to the South during Reconstruction
  - breaking down the events in a biography
- Math
  - preparing descriptions of algebraic proofs
  - constructing word problems
- ELA
  - organizing book reports
  - unifying a five paragraph essay
  - writing a formal letter
  - organizing note-taking for an essay

Secondary School

- Science
  - taking notes for a lab report
  - describing changes of state
  - defining the process of erosion
- Social Studies
  - converting census data to sociological trends
  - tracing cultural heritage through migration
  - creating an eyewitness account of historical fiction
- Math
  - breaking down a multi-stage proof in calculus
  - applying math to observed chemical phenomena
- ELA
  - writing a synopsis of a novel
  - converting a short story into a drama

- ○ outlining a proclamation
- ○ proving a theory about an author

Common Core State Standards

College and Career Readiness Anchor Standards for Writing

Text Types and Purposes

1. Write arguments to support claims in an analysis of substantive topics or texts, using valid reasoning and relevant and sufficient evidence.

2. Write informative/explanatory texts to examine and convey complex ideas and information clearly and accurately through the effective selection, organization, and analysis of content.

3. Write narratives to develop real or imagined experiences or events using effective technique, well-chosen details, and well-structured event sequences.

Production and Distribution of Writing

4. Produce clear and coherent writing in which the development, organization, and style are appropriate to task, purpose, and audience.

5. Develop and strengthen writing as needed by planning, revising, editing, rewriting, or trying a new approach.

Teaching the Strategy

Introduce the strategy by explaining that a thesis statement has two parts: topic + (your opinion) = a thesis statement:

The children of people in prison (need time with their parents).

- **Limited Topic.** In a short essay, you can't discuss the history of the world. Stick to a topic that can be successfully covered in a few paragraphs.

- **Precise Opinion.** Writers who are focused will offer an opinion that can be backed up by evidence and reasons gathered from their research.

Thesis Statement Rules

- **Usually comes first.** In most types of writing, you want the reader to address the core issue or controlling idea in the first paragraph and begin thinking about it. The thesis does not usually appear in the first sentence, which tends to be an interest–grabber. Instead of stating the thesis first, you might present some evidence for them to think about before you include your thesis statement as a summary to the first paragraph.

- **Significant and general.** The thesis statement contains larger ideas and sweeping statements while the other sentences in a paragraph present facts or ideas that are only part of the broader topic sentence.

- **Controlling ideas, not facts.** A good thesis statement needs to be further explained; the reader wants to know more. Supporting sentences present details that stand on their own and don't need an explanation.

- **Avoid personal opinions.** Readers aren't that interested in what the writer thinks. Avoid saying, "I like . . . " or "I think . . . ." Let the facts speak for themselves.

- **Express intent and a provable opinion.** Strong writers indicate what they will accomplish with their work. They know readers will react to reliable information. They are presenting their opinions in order to change a reader's opinion.

- **Interest the reader.** Thesis statements should provoke and intrigue the reader and make them want to continue reading.

- **Restrictive and carefully worded.** Readers should be able to determine the main idea easily and not be left wondering what to think.

- **Act as a bridge.** The topic sentences of subsequent paragraphs connect ideas and lead readers from one point to another. An essay's overall thesis statement unites the topic sentences as well.

- **Not a title or an explanation.** A thesis statement is more than just a main idea. A title expresses a main idea and is intended to summarize a piece of writing.

The methodology for constructing thesis statements involves moving from the general to the specific. Note the one-word starting topic below and how it is refined into a limited topic and then fully expressed as an opinion or an intention as the final thesis statement.

- **Starting Topic:** Basketball
- **Limited Topic:** Lessons about life learned from basketball
- **Thesis Statement:** If I hadn't played basketball, I would have been far less successful in life.

This same process is followed when converting the ideas and facts of research into a thesis statement that will present to the reader the evidence that has been gathered.

Directed Writing Activity

1. This activity will require students to produce clear and coherent writing in which development, organization, and style are appropriate to task and purpose. Use the ideas and facts in this list to formulate a suitable thesis statement for an introductory paragraph that someone could write using these sentences.

2. Display the list on the chalkboard, whiteboard, or overhead. Then have students define what these sentences have in common and articulate how they are related.

3. Ask students to suggest ideas in the form of a starting topic.

4. Students should then suggest a possible limited topic for a paragraph containing these sentences. Ask them to explain their thinking as they make these suggestions by noting information in the sentences that leads them there.

5. Finally, have students write possible thesis statements and then critique their suggestions before finally agreeing on a topic.

   A. If players on offense are kept off balance and uncomfortable, they tend to score less.

   B. If your opposition scores fewer points, you don't have to score as many points either.

   C. Any player can provide solid defense while very few players can score at will.

   D. A team that wins every game can often score less on a given night by playing defense.

6. Look at the facts presented in these sentences:
   - Sentence A discusses players scoring less.
   - Sentence B talks about scoring less.
   - Sentence C discusses defense.
   - Sentence D talks about defense.

7. Overall, each sentence mentions defense and why it is crucial if a team expects to win. In writing a thesis statement, the writer has to link these ideas while making a larger point. Have students define the starting topic and formulate a limited topic from the sentences. Use these as a starting point.
   - **Starting Topic:** Basketball
   - **Limited Topic:** Playing defense and offense in basketball

8. Now work with students to develop a sentence that will serve as a thesis statement. Use the example below and show how it incorporates and restates all the ideas of the sentences.
   - **Thesis statement:** The key to victory in basketball is defense, not offense.

   This statement links success with defense and values defense over offense. This reflects the ideas put forth in the other sentences of the paragraph but notice that it isn't just a fact or detail. Its ideas apply to all the other sentences and the ideas they contain.

9. Have students share their thesis statements and have them justify how theirs serves to introduce the paragraph or essay.

10. Assign the independent writing activity.

Reference

Jones, R. *Rigor and Relevance Handbook*. Rexford, NY: International Center for Leadership in Education, 2010.

For the Student

Independent Writing Activity

Now have students complete the worksheet. Reproduce and hand it out to them or display it on the chalkboard, whiteboard, or overhead. They should develop their writing appropriately by planning, revising, and editing.

1. Students should read the first two paragraphs and determine what ideas and facts they share.

2. Students should follow the topic → limited topic → thesis statement format to generate an appropriate topic sentence for each paragraph.

3. For the two sandwich diagrams on the bottom of the sheet, students should follow the directions to develop ideas and facts for a narrative paragraph of their own choosing.

4. Students will then write paragraphs with appropriate thesis statements using the ideas and facts they developed.

Thesis Statement Worksheets

Directions: Use the information in each paragraph to write a suitable thesis statement. Begin by providing the Starting Topic and Limited Topic.

Paragraph 1

Starting Topic: _____

Limited Topic: _____

Thesis Statement: _____

In Latin, the term *briba* meant a piece of bread given to beggars but in modern English it has passed through meaning everything from alms, blackmail and extortion, to gifts received or given in order to influence corruptly. People give bribes to someone as payment to do what really ought to be done out of a conscientious sense of duty. A person who takes a bribe is said to be corrupted, and thus corruption is a term sometimes held equivalent to bribery. The purification of the bench from judicial bribery has been gradual, with the earliest recorded case was that of England's Sir William Thorpe, who in 1351 was fined and removed from office for accepting bribes. There is, perhaps, no other crime on which the force of law, if unaided by public opinion and morals, can have so little influence; for in other crimes, such as violence or fraud, there is generally some person immediately injured by the act, who can give his aid in the detection of the offender, but in the perpetration of the offence of bribery all the immediate parties obtain what they desire, and are satisfied.

Starting Topic: _____

Limited Topic: _____

Thesis Statement: _____

_____

In spite of their external similarity, electric eels have nothing to do with nonelectric eels. Other than the fact that they resemble the latter in terms of their elongated body, the large number of vertebrae, and the absence of pelvic fins, they differ in all the more important characters of internal structure. They are, in fact, allied to the carps and the catfishes with which they share a chain of small bones. A structure of so complicated and specialized an apparatus can only be the result of a community of descent of the families possessing it. The animal's electric organs extend the whole length of the tail, which is four-fifths of the body. They are modifications of the lateral muscles and are supplied with numerous branches of the spinal nerves. They consist of longitudinal columns, each composed of an immense number of "electric plates." The posterior end of the organ is positive, the anterior negative, and the current passes from the tail to the head. The maximum shock is given when the head and tail are in contact with different points in the surface of some other animal. If forced to use their electric shock again and again, electric eels become defenseless and can only regain this power after a long rest.

Sandwich Paragraphs Worksheets

Write three sentences for each "sandwich" paragraph. First, state facts or ideas you would use in a paragraph that describes a childhood memory. Then, write another paragraph that tells something interesting about a friend or a relative. These sentences will form the "meat, cheese, lettuce, and pickles" of your sandwiches. Then you will write a thesis statement for each that introduces and unites each set of sentences into a paragraph. Write the thesis statement in the piece of bread on top. For the piece of bread on the bottom, write a conclusion that fits the thesis statement.

Childhood Memory Sandwich

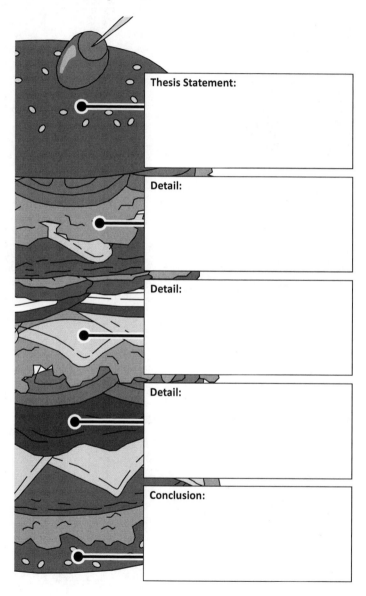

Thesis Statement:

Detail:

Detail:

Detail:

Conclusion:

Friend or Relative Revelation

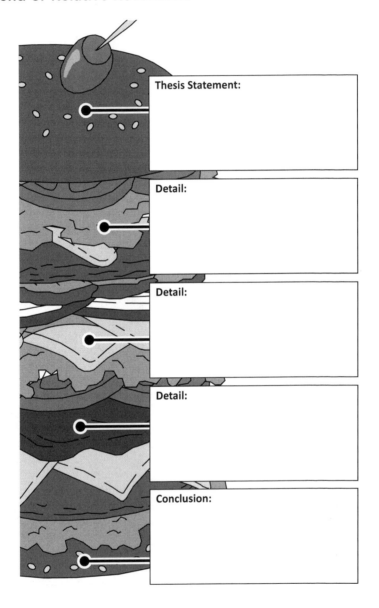

Thesis Statement:

Detail:

Detail:

Detail:

Conclusion:

# Writing Frames

For the Teacher

Defining the Strategy

Every good piece of writing begins with an outline. The outline provides a road map for the writing. Writing frames are similar to outlines, but they are made up of incomplete sentences. Rather than focusing on the structure of a piece of writing, writing frames allow the student to focus on what they want to convey in their writing by means of scaffolding specific to the type of writing.

Students may use this strategy for writing many different types of texts, however, the Common Core State Standards emphasize argument writing in particular. As such, this strategy will focus on writing frames for arguments. One helpful aspect of writing frames is that they can be adjusted to provide different levels of scaffolding. Writing frames help students to convey complex ideas and information clearly and accurately. They also help students develop and organize their writing while finding a style that is appropriate for their purpose and audience.

The objective of writing frames is to provide scaffolding for students. These frames require learners to use their knowledge — both to analyze and solve problems and to create solutions. In terms of student performance, the use of writing frames fits within Quadrant B (Application) on the Rigor/Relevance Framework.

Applying the Strategy

While the use of writing frames to assist in writing arguments is the focus of this strategy, writing frames can also be used for narrative writing and informative/explanatory writing. The strategy aligns well with standards 1, 8, and 9 of the Common Core College and Career Anchor Standards for Writing.

Standard 1 relates specifically to argument writing and supporting claims with valid reasoning and sufficient evidence. A writing frame can be used to ensure that a piece of writing does exactly this — states a claim and supports it with evidence.

Standard 8 relates to the gathering of information and the inclusion of that information in a piece of writing, all while avoiding plagiarism. It is extremely important that students are taught how to avoid plagiarism. Writing frames can show students how to take information and put it into their own words.

Standard 9 covers drawing evidence from literary or informational texts to support analysis, reflection, and research. A writing frame can help students organize this evidence to support their ideas.

Writing frames are an effective strategy that can be used in nearly every content area in middle and secondary schools.

Middle School

- Science
    - summarizing a scientific concept
    - writing about experiments
    - drawing conclusions
- Social Studies
    - writing fact and opinion essays
    - analyzing historical events

- Math
  - describing mathematical properties, operations, and proofs
- ELA
  - organizing concepts, ideas, and information
  - developing topics

Secondary School

- Science
  - refuting other claims
  - drawing conclusions
  - summarizing scientific processes
- Social Studies
  - writing essays, writing opinion-based and research-based papers
- Math
  - writing mathematical arguments in proofs
  - describing mathematical solutions
- ELA
  - developing a topic with well-chosen, relevant, and sufficient facts
  - stating opinions
  - forming an argument

Common Core State Standards

College and Career Readiness Anchor Standards for Writing

Text Types and Purposes

1. Write arguments to support claims in an analysis of substantive topics or texts using valid reasoning and relevant and sufficient evidence.

2. Write informative/explanatory texts to examine and convey complex ideas and information clearly and accurately through the effective selection, organization, and analysis of content.

3. Write narratives to develop real or imagined experiences or events using effective technique, well-chosen details and well-structured event sequences.

Production and Distribution of Writing

4. Produce clear and coherent writing in which the development, organization, and style are appropriate to task, purpose, and audience.

5. Develop and strengthen writing as needed by planning, revising, editing, rewriting, or trying a new approach.

Research to Build and Present Knowledge

8. Gather relevant information from multiple print and digital sources, assess the credibility and accuracy of each source, and integrate the information while avoiding plagiarism.

9. Draw evidence from literary or informational texts to support analysis, reflection, and research.

Teaching the Strategy

Briefly review the concept of writing an argument with students. Then introduce the strategy by presenting the basic writing frame below.

After learning about the issues surrounding _____ (topic), I agree/disagree/am convinced that _____ (your claim). One reason for my position is _____ (first reason for your claim).

The purposes of a writing frame include:

- **To provide structure**. A writing frame can be used to provide the expected structure of a piece of writing. In the example above, the writing frame provides the structure for the beginning of an argument. Using the writing frame ensures that students become used to the structure and formalities of writing an argument.

- **To use transitions to connect ideas.** A writing frame is an excellent way to introduce academic language that students can use as they transition from one idea to the next in a piece of writing. The words and phrases in a writing frame help students to state their perspectives, cite text-based evidence, and discuss counterclaims.

- **To encourage personal interpretation.** A writing frame can encourage writers to think more deeply about a topic and form their opinions. It can pose questions that help them show their understanding.

Writing models are useful, important tools for learning how to use academic language as a writer. Writing frames model writing conventions by giving students examples of how to write transitions, opinions, reasons, and so on. Eventually, students will be able to call on these strategies with less guidance as they grow in their writing and their work.

Writing frames exist in many formats. Since their main purpose is to scaffold writing, they can be modified as necessary for specific levels. Beginning writers may need more text in a writing frame, while an advanced writer should have less and less text. Writing frames can be constructed to be very specific or relatively vague. The table below gives suggestions for writing frames.

Writing Frames

Purpose	Grades K–5 Frames	Grades 6–12 Frames
• To introduce ideas	• This book tells us that ____. • People say that ____.	• A number of ____ have suggested that ____. • It is often said that ____. • Many people assume that ____. • In this text about ____, the author claims that ____.
• To respond to text	• I agree with the author that ____. • Unlike the author, I believe that ____.	• I (support/endorse) the speaker's conclusion that ____. • I disagree with the author because research shows that ____. • The author's claim rests on the mistaken assumption that ____. • Although the author is correct that ____, I disagree with the notion that ____.

Writing Frames (Continued)

Purpose	Grades K–5 Frames	Grades 6–12 Frames
To distinguish points of view	• The author believes that ____, but I think ____. • I disagree with the author. She believes that ____. I believe that ____.	• Although the author says ____, I believe that ____. • The speaker argues that ____, but in my opinion, ____. • The author is mistaken about ____; instead, I would argue that ____. • The speaker is correct in saying that ____. In addition, I would add that ____.
To make a counterclaim	• Other people might argue that ____. • Some readers might think that ____.	• Some critics might believe ____, but I would argue that ____. • Opponents of ____ claim that ____, but evidence indicates that ____. • A common assumption about ____ is ____. However, I am convinced that ____.
To conclude	• This matters because ____. • We should care about this because ____. • ____ should support ____ because ____.	• ____ is important because ____. • Overwhelming evidence has led me to conclude that ____. • Ultimately, this issue of ____ affects ____.

Do be aware, though, that writing frames can be overused. Hence, appropriate scaffolding and modification are always important. If you see that your students are not stretching their thinking, but simply filling in the blanks, move to a more general writing frame that helps them to find structure without holding them back. Alternatively, allow them to fill in the blanks for their first writing, but require them to step back from the blanks for their next writing.

Directed Writing Activity

1. This activity will require students to use a writing frame to respond to an address to Parliament by Winston Churchill in 1940. The writing frame will help students produce clear and coherent writing in which development, organization, and style are suited to the task and purpose of the piece. Students should integrate information from the text into their argument.

2. Distribute copies of the text "Blood, Toil, Tears, and Sweat: Address to Parliament on May 13th, 1940" by Winston Churchill. Ask students to read the address twice.

3. Then distribute copies of the writing frame to students. Ask the following questions about the writing frame to help students become familiar with it:

   - What does the writer say Churchill is claiming?

   - Where does the writer quote the author?

   - Where does the writer state a claim?

   - Where does the writer present a counterclaim?

4. Next, give students time to complete the writing frame. When they are finished, invite several students to share their work with the class. Discuss how even though everyone used the same writing frame, students' writing came out differently.

5. Engage students in a conversation regarding the use of writing frames, what they found most helpful, what they found constraining, and so on. Point out that they can use more generic writing frames, if they wish, to help them begin any kind of writing. The writing frame does not need to be as specific as this one was.

6. Assign the independent writing activity.

Reference

Marzano, R. et al. *Classroom Instruction That Works*. Alexandria, VA: ASCD, 2001.

Writing Frame for Directed Writing Activity

In his 1940 speech to Parliament, Winston Churchill claims that war is

_____. He states, "_____."

Although it is true that _____, I believe that

_____. My opinion is based on _____

_____ and _____. Of course, Europeans

in 1940 might say that _____, but today,

_____. My opinion about _____

could also apply to _____.

Sample Writing Frame

In his 1940 speech to Parliament, Winston Churchill claims that war is inevitable and necessary. He states, "We have before us many, many months of struggling and suffering." Although it is true that Hitler was a terrible threat, I believe that war is rarely inevitable. My opinion is based on our experiences in Vietnam and Iraq. Of course, Europeans in 1940 might say that Nazism was an obvious threat, but today, we seem to choose our wars instead of having them forced on us. My opinion about the false inevitability of war could also apply to conflicts in Africa and the Middle East.

Blood, Toil, Tears, and Sweat: Address to Parliament on May 13th, 1940

by Winston Churchill

I say to the House as I said to ministers who have joined this government, I have nothing to offer but blood, toil, tears, and sweat. We have before us an ordeal of the most grievous kind. We have before us many, many months of struggle and suffering.

You ask, what is our policy? I say it is to wage war by land, sea, and air. War with all our might and with all the strength God has given us, and to wage war against a monstrous tyranny never surpassed in the dark and lamentable catalogue of human crime. That is our policy.

You ask, what is our aim? I can answer in one word. It is victory. Victory at all costs—Victory in spite of all terrors—Victory, however long and hard the road may be, for without victory there is no survival.

I take up my task in buoyancy and hope. I feel sure that our cause will not be suffered to fail among men. I feel entitled at this juncture, at this time, to claim the aid of all and to say, "Come then, let us go forward together with our united strength."

For the Student

Independent Writing Activity

Follow these directions to write an argument in response to a piece of writing. You will use a writing frame to help you develop your writing appropriately in the planning stage. Once you have completed the writing frame, you can revise and edit your writing to be sure you have included sufficient evidence to support your argument.

1. Read the excerpt of Elie Wiesel's Nobel Peace Prize acceptance speech.

2. Complete the writing frame to craft a response to the speech.

3. How did the writing frame help you in the writing process?

Sample answer: It helped me to organize my writing and to make sure I included reasons and sufficient evidence.

4. Refine your writing by revising and editing.

Sample Writing Frame

In his speech to the Nobel Committee, Elie Wiesel suggests that he does not deserve the honor. He questions whether he is worthy, and asks, "Do I have the right?" Although Wiesel is correct that no one may speak for the dead, I believe that he deserves the honor because he has at least tried to do so. Some survivors might object to my argument that Wiesel is worthy of the prize, but I am convinced that his writings and struggles have kept their history in the public eye for decades. My feelings about Wiesel might also apply to any writer who tries to keep an injustice from vanishing from history.

Hope, Despair, and Memory

by Elie Wiesel

It is with a profound sense of humility that I accept the honor—the highest there is—that you have chosen to bestow on me. I know your choice transcends my person.

Do I have the right to represent the multitudes who have perished? Do I have the right to accept this great honor on their behalf? I do not. No one may speak for the dead, no one may interpret their mutilated dreams and visions. And yet, I sense their presence. I always do—and at this moment more than ever. The presence of my parents, that of my little sister. The presence of my teachers, my friends, my companions . . . .

This honor belongs to all the survivors and their children, and, through us, to the Jewish people with whose destiny I have always identified.

I remember: it happened yesterday, or eternities ago. A young Jewish boy discovered the Kingdom of Night. I remember his bewilderment, I remember his anguish. It all happened so fast. The ghetto. The deportation. The sealed cattle car. The fiery altar upon which the history of our people and the future of mankind were meant to be sacrificed.

I remember he asked his father: "Can this be true? This is the twentieth century, not the Middle Ages. Who would allow such crimes to be committed? How could the world remain silent?"

And now the boy is turning to me. "Tell me," he asks, "what have you done with my future, what have you done with your life?" And I tell him that I have tried. That I have tried to keep memory alive, that I have tried to fight those who would forget. Because if we forget, we are guilty, we are accomplices.

And then I explain to him how naïve we were, that the world did know and remained silent. And that is why I swore never to be silent whenever, wherever human beings endure suffering and humiliation. We must take sides. Neutrality helps the oppressor, never the victim. Silence encourages the tormentor, never the tormented. Sometimes we must interfere. When human lives are endangered, when human dignity is in jeopardy, national borders and sensitivities become irrelevant. Wherever men and women are persecuted because of their race, religion, or political views, that place must — at that moment — become the center of the universe.

Writing Frame for Independent Writing Activity

In his speech to the Nobel Committee, Elie Wiesel suggests that

_____. He questions whether _____,

and asks, "_____?" Although Wiesel is correct that

_____, I believe that _____ because

_____. Some _____

_____ might object to my argument that _____,

but I am convinced that _____. My feelings

about _____ might also apply to _____

_____.

Writing Process: Prewriting

Defining the Strategy

When faced with the challenge of starting a writing project, many students will think, *I don't have any ideas! Where do I start? How can I organize my thinking?* Prewriting is a way to discover and develop a topic for writing. When learners prewrite, they explore ideas and topics, discover details, and examine subjects that they need or want to research further. This enables them to produce clear and coherent writing in which the development, organization, and style are appropriate to task, purpose, and audience.

The objective of prewriting is to focus and organize rigorous and relevant thinking. As they prewrite, learners find ways to start and structure their writing. Prewriting fits within Quadrant A on the Rigor/Relevance Framework, giving learners the tools to move forward to work in the other quadrants of the framework.

Applying the Strategy

Prewriting is a useful tool for any writing assignment in middle school or high school. The skill can help students in these subject areas:

- Science: choosing a topic and exploring research options
- Social Studies: finding relevant ideas and details
- Math: arranging and categorizing statistics
- ELA: collecting and organizing details and descriptions

Common Core State Standards

College and Career Readiness Anchor Standards for Writing

Text Types and Purposes

2. Write arguments to support claims in an analysis of substantive topics or texts, using valid reasoning and relevant and sufficient evidence.

Production and Distribution of Writing

5. Develop and strengthen writing as needed by planning, revising, editing, rewriting, or trying a new approach.

Teaching the Strategy

Introduce the strategy by explaining that the main purposes of prewriting are:

- **To generate and clarify ideas.** Prewriting can aid learners in focusing their thinking, and in helping them to choose and narrow a topic that is relevant to their writing assignment. For example, an assignment might ask students to write a research paper on the Roman Empire. Prewriting can help students generate ideas about the Roman Empire and choose one that interests them, such as the fall of Rome.

- **To organize ideas.** Prewriting can help students understand more clearly which ideas and details are best suited for inclusion in a writing assignment and the best way to organize them. For the assignment on the fall of Rome, prewriting can help students decide whether to organize the facts and details they find by chronology, order of importance, or another order.

Generating Ideas

Before learners even begin coming up with ideas, they should ask themselves two questions:

- **What is my purpose?** Purposes for writing can include writing *to inform, to persuade, to evaluate,* or *to entertain.* Some writing combines two or more of these purposes. Determining purpose can help writers decide on the best way to organize their writing.

- **Who is my audience?** Some writing, for instance research papers, is done for a teacher. The audience for an article, though, might be newspaper or magazine readers. The audience for a blog could be people the writer's own age. Determining audience can help writers decide on the tone and language to use in their writing.

It is important that students understand their purpose for writing and be aware of their audience. Provide frames like these to help students articulate their research and writing purpose and to identify their audience.

- I am conducting research on _____ for an audience that includes _____.

- I hope to learn because _____.

- In this (product) _____, my goal is to _____ my audience (about/that) _____.

There are several techniques students can use to generate ideas. These include:

1. **Brainstorming.** Brainstorming uses mental association to create a list of ideas and details that are linked to a topic. Here are the steps to use in brainstorming:
   - Write down a general topic.
   - Quickly jot down all the ideas and words you can think of that are linked to the topic.
   - When the list is complete, group linked items and label each group. Each group becomes a possible writing topic.

Brainstorming can be used by individual learners or groups. It is useful for any kind of writing assignment.

2. **Clustering.** Clustering also uses association to generate and link ideas and details. To cluster, follow these steps:

    - Write a general topic in the center of a piece of paper and circle it.

    - Think of ideas and details that connect to the topic. Circle each and draw a line to the central topic.

    - Continue writing down ideas and details that connect to the new ideas. Circle them and draw lines to link them to the new ideas.

    Clustering helps to show relationships among ideas. It can help students identify which topics most interest them. Those will usually be the ideas in the cluster with the greatest number of links. Clustering is especially useful for planning essays, persuasive writing, and narrative writing.

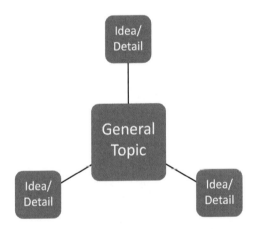

3. **QuickWrite Routine**. The QuickWrite Routine guides students to reflect on new information in order to connect reading with learning. It is important to use this routine after students have interacted with the text multiple times and demonstrated an understanding of its ideas before they are asked to form a view-

point about the topic. This is a key expectation in the Common Core State Standards. Students then use this routine to support their viewpoints using text-based evidence.

- **Brainstorm ideas**. Students use a list or a graphic organizer such as a concept web to reflect on, and record ideas about, an issue in the text. Helpful frames to guide students might include: "One thing I learned from the text about this issue is _____" and "An idea that is important to me is _____."

- **Take a position.** Students determine their positions on the subject and articulate their viewpoints using sentence starters such as "My position on this topic is _____" or "I (agree/disagree) with this idea because _____."

- **Support your viewpoint.** Students locate evidence from the text to support their viewpoints. You can provide students with frames such as "My viewpoint is _____. I hold this perspective because _____. One piece of evidence from the text that supports my viewpoint is _____."

- **Write your response to the text.** Allow students five minutes to combine the frames from the first steps to write their responses to the text topic.

4. **Questioning.** Questioning uses the 5 Ws and 1 H to explore and deepen thought about a topic. Ask these questions:

- Who? Write down who is involved and who is affected.

- What? Write down what happens.

- Where? Write down where the action occurs or has an effect.

- When? Write down when the action happened and when it must be addressed.

- Why? Write down why the problem occurred and why it is important.

- How? Write down how the problem is addressed or solved.

The 5 Ws and 1 H are often known as journalists' questions. They are especially useful for planning articles and essays.

Organizing Information

Once students have decided on their purpose, audience, and topic, they can gather material for their writing and start to organize it. There are several methods for organizing writing details. These methods can help students organize ideas, concepts, and information, using strategies such as definition, classification, comparison/contrast, and cause/effect.

1. **Story Pyramid.** A story pyramid contains eight lines inside a pyramid shape. It can help learners generate ideas and details about a story's characters, setting, and plot. To create a story pyramid, follow these steps:

    *   Draw a triangle.
    *   On line 1, at the top, write a single word naming the main character.
    *   On line 2, write two words describing the character.
    *   On line 3, write three words describing the setting.
    *   On line 4, write four words explaining the problem.
    *   On line 5, write five words describing one event.
    *   On line 6, write six words describing the second event.
    *   On line 7, write seven words describing the third event.
    *   On line 8, write eight words explaining the solution to the problem.

    Story pyramids are useful for planning a nonfiction or fiction narrative.

2. **Events Chain** or **Flow Chart.** These charts show how events proceed over time. They can be used in science writing to organize details about an experiment, or in social studies writing to organize dates and events. They are also useful in writing instructions or directions. In fiction writing, an events chain can help organize the plot in time-sequence order. To use an events chain, write one event in each box.

3. **Problem-Solution Diagrams**. These charts help writers organize problems and solutions. They are especially useful for fiction, essay, or article writing. To use a problem-solution chart, write

down the main problems at the top. Then write possible solutions and details about the solutions.

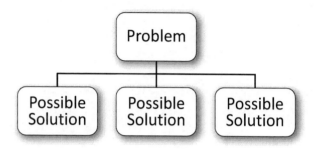

4. **Comparison-Contrast Charts** and **Venn Diagrams**. These graphic aids help writers see the differences and similarities in the topics they are comparing and contrasting. They can be used in most kinds of nonfiction writing. To use these graphic aids, write down details that are the same and different in the appropriate columns or sections of the graphic.

5. **Cycle Chart**. These charts show events that occur in cycles. They are especially useful in science writing, for instance, to organize information on topics such as the water cycle or the nitrogen cycle. To use a cycle chart, write one step of the cycle in each section or box.

6. **Outline**. An outline organizes information in headings and subheadings. It is useful for any kind of nonfiction writing. To create an outline, use Roman numerals for main headings. Indicate subheadings with capital letters. Supporting details require numbers.

I. Main Heading
    A. Subheading
    B. Subheading
        1. Supporting details
        2. Supporting details
        3. Supporting details

Directed Writing Activity

1. This activity will require students to develop and strengthen writing by planning. Give students a broad problem on which to write an editorial. Some possibilities include: a local environmental issue, a local or national election, or a problem related to the school.

2. Distribute the cluster diagram form to students.

3. Discuss the purpose and audience for the editorial. Which newspaper is the target – a school paper? A local paper? An online paper? Will the editorial attempt to persuade people to think or act in a certain way?

4. Ask students to fill in the center of the diagram with the topic you've chosen. Then encourage students to use the clustering technique to continue filling in the form, adding additional circles if necessary.

5. Develop a class clustering form with student help. Discuss which topics seem most suitable for the purpose and audience you've discussed.

6. Assign the organizing activity.

Sample Cluster Form

Organizing Activity

Follow these directions to organize your ideas for an editorial. Plan an editorial that supports claims with clear reasons and relevant evidence.

1. Use the topic you chose in the clustering activity.

2. Complete a problem-solution chart describing the problem you have chosen and possible solutions. Include reasons and evidence in your chart. Add boxes if necessary.

Sample Problem-Solution Diagram

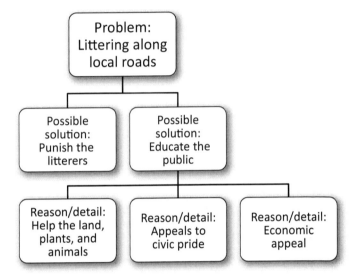

For the Student

Cluster Diagram

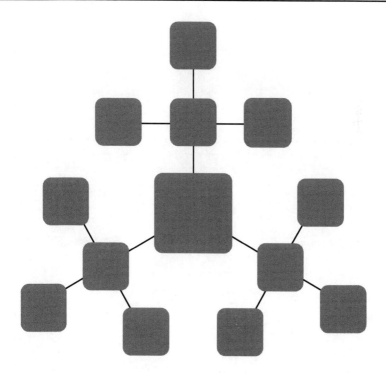

Problem-Solution Diagram

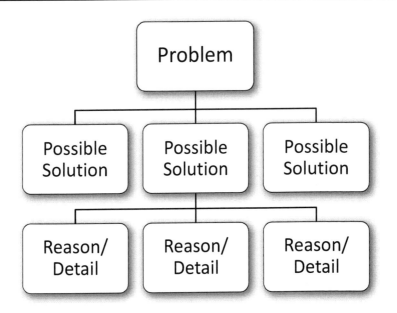

◼ Writing Process: Drafting

For the Teacher

Defining the Strategy

Once students have chosen a topic, found facts and details about the topic, and organized their information, they are ready to write. Sometimes facing the blank first page can be as unnerving as coming up with a writing idea. Drafting is a way for writers to get their ideas down on paper without worrying too much about style, grammar, or punctuation. It is the first step in writing both over extended time frames (time for research, reflection, and revision) and shorter time frames (a single sitting or a day or two) for a range of tasks, purposes, and audiences.

The objective of drafting is to use rigorous and relevant thinking to get ideas onto paper. Drafting fits within Quadrants B and C on the Rigor/Relevance Framework, giving learners the opportunity to use, extend, and refine the information they have found.

Applying the Strategy

For any writing assignment in middle school or high school, drafting is the first actual writing step. This skill is a required part of writing in most content areas in middle and secondary programs.

- Science:
  - a research paper on tides or the water cycle
- Social Studies
  - an essay on the causes of the Civil War
  - an article on the Jamestown Colony
- Math
  - an explanation of a survey
  - an essay explaining a math concept to a younger audience
- ELA
  - a one-act play based on a Greek myth
  - a newspaper article about a local election

Common Core State Standards

College and Career Readiness Anchor Standards for Writing

Text Types and Purposes

1. Write arguments to support claims in an analysis of substantive topics or texts, using valid reasoning and relevant and sufficient evidence.

Production and Distribution of Writing

4. Produce clear and coherent writing in which the development, organization, and style are appropriate to task, purpose, and audience.

5. Develop and strengthen writing as needed by planning, revising, editing, rewriting, or trying a new approach.

Range of Writing

10. Write routinely over extended time frames (time for research, reflection, and revision) and shorter time frames (a single sitting or a day or two) for a range of tasks, purposes, and audiences.

Teaching the Strategy

Introduce the strategy by describing the main sections of a draft:

- **The introduction**. In a nonfiction piece of writing, this includes the topic sentence or thesis sentence. In fiction, this section might introduce the main character and describe the setting.

- **The body.** In nonfiction, this section includes main ideas and details. In fiction, it introduces the problem and focuses on the main events.

- **The conclusion.** In nonfiction, the conclusion summarizes the main arguments or points. In fiction, it describes the solution to the problem and brings the action to a close.

Introduction: Nonfiction

The introduction to a piece of nonfiction writing should do the following:

1. Introduce the purpose of the paper in a topic or thesis statement. A strong thesis statement does the following:
   - It takes a stand.
   - It is specific.
   - It addresses one main idea.

Here are sample weak and strong thesis statements:

- **Weak:** Placing a carbon tax on airline flights is something many governments are considering.
- **Strong**: Carbon taxes on airline flights are a good way to try to fight global warming.

A thesis statement can appear at any point in the first paragraph of the introduction.

2. Give the audience a sense of how the argument will develop. Include key concepts and ideas.

3. Provide context to show why the main idea is significant. Include your purpose for writing.

Introduction: Narrative Writing

The introduction to a narrative should do the following:
1. Grab the readers' attention.

2. Introduce the main character or characters.

3. Describe the setting.

4. Introduce the problem or conflict.

   Here are examples of a weak and strong narrative introduction:

   - **Weak**: It was a day in late July. It was very hot and quiet. The sun beat down on the city streets and melted the tar. Suddenly there was an enormous explosion.
   - **Strong**: Jasmin walked down the center of the deserted, steamy street, popping tar bubbles with her flipflops. The air was almost too hot to breathe. Without warning came a blast of sound so strong it threw Jasmin to the ground.

Body: Nonfiction

The body in a piece of nonfiction writing will include arguments, facts, and details that the writer has first gathered in research and then organized in prewriting. Each paragraph in the body should include a topic sentence stating the paragraph's main idea and supporting details. As well, paragraphs should employ transitions to show how one idea is linked to the next.

Body: Narrative Writing

The body of a piece of narrative writing develops the plot and characters, telling how the main character addresses the problem or conflict. The action will rise to a climax when the main character faces and tries to solve the problem or conflict.

Conclusion: Nonfiction

The purpose of a nonfiction conclusion is to restate and elaborate on the argument. There are several ways to do this:

- **Return to the ideas in the introduction.** This strategy brings the reader full circle. You may also refer to the introductory paragraph by using key words or parallel concepts and images that you used in the introduction.

- **Synthesize your ideas.** Include a brief summary of the paper's main points, and show your reader how the points you made fit together with the support and examples you used.

- **Propose a course of action, a solution to an issue, or questions for further study.** This can redirect readers' thoughts and help them either apply your ideas to their own lives or see the broader implications of your view.

Conclusion: Narrative Writing

The conclusion to a narrative should explain how the main problem or conflict has been resolved. Some possibilities for a strong conclusion include:

- an anecdote/scenario describing a situation that reiterates or illustrates the point
- a prediction, i.e., a statement of what may result from the situation discussed in the writing
- a question that stimulates further thought in the reader
- a reflection that helps the reader understand the main point or message of the narrative

Directed Writing Activity

1. This activity will require students to produce clear and coherent writing in which the development, organization, and style are appropriate to task, purpose, and audience. For this activity, they will write the introduction to an editorial.

2. Have students look back at the problem-solution diagram they filled out in the prewriting activity.

3. Pass out copies of the drafting organizer. Have students consider the purpose and audience they chose in the prewriting activity.

4. Ask students to write an introduction to their editorial. Remind them to take a stand and include only one main idea, and to write quickly without worrying about spelling or punctuation.

5. Develop a class introduction for an editorial. Encourage students to contribute ideas to make the introduction strong.

Purpose: to persuade

Audience: local online newspaper readers

Introduction: Littering is a huge problem in our area. The roads are covered with garbage. People toss fast-food wrappers out car windows. They toss soda cans. They toss old tires and clothing. It is necessary that something is done. I believe our best option is educating the public.

---

6. After learners complete their introductions, review and discuss the assignment. Encourage students to read aloud their work and talk about whether the introductions introduce a claim and organize the reasons and evidence clearly.

7. Assign the independent writing activity. Review the three parts of a draft: introduction, body, and conclusion. Remind students that when they draft, they should write quickly without paying too much attention to spelling or punctuation. Then ask them to write the rest of a draft of their editorial to support claims with clear reasons and relevant evidence, using credible sources and demonstrating an understanding of the topic.

For the Student

Independent Writing Activity

Follow these directions to draft your editorial, writing arguments to support claims in an analysis of substantive topics or texts, using valid reasoning and relevant and sufficient evidence.

1. Use the introduction you wrote for the directed writing activity.

2. In the drafting organizer, write a body for your editorial. Outline the problem and elaborate on your solution. Write arguments to support claims with clear reasons and relevant evidence.

3. Write a conclusion for your narrative that provides a concluding statement or section that follows from the argument presented.

Drafting Organizer

Title:

Main character:

Setting:

Introduction:

Body:

Conclusion:

Sample Drafting Organizer

Purpose: to persuade

Audience: local online newspaper readers

Introduction: Littering is a huge problem in Yarborough. The roads are covered with garbage. People toss fast-food wrapers out car windows. They toss soda cans. They toss old tires and clothing. It is necessary that something is done. I believe our best option is educating the public.

Body: If people knew the affects of littering on the economy and the environment, they would be less likely to toss their trash. The things they throw out hurt the land plants and animals. Old tires and electronics! They can be toxic. Animals eat plastic refuse. They get tangled in it. Many people don't know this, however. In the event that there were more information available about the effects of littering on the land and living creatures, littering would be less likely to be done by people.

We can also appeal to people's civick pride. People like their towns to look nice. Milltown looks much nicer than our town. It's not nice to see all that grungy junk along our roads and in our streams and meadows. If people was aware of how others look at our town, they might feel ashamed and embarrassed—and they might be willing to work to stop the problem. There is the economic cost of littering. Our town gets a lot of it's income from tourists. Tourists don't want to look at litter. It follows, then, that litter has the ability to hurt people's incomes. The hotel and motel restaurant and shop owners will all benefit from a program to stop litter. Letting him know how much litter costs them in business will make them more willing to support the effort.

Conclusion:

It is clear to see that educating the public be the best way to address the problem of littering in our town. It would be impossible to catch all the people doing the littering. We need to get townspeople to police the problem—and to stop doing it when they are the problem. An education program about littering will help to take our town from disgusting to delightful.

Writing Process: Editing

For the Teacher

Defining the Strategy

Learners might think that running a spellcheck program on their writing work is enough editing. But a spellcheck program wouldn't change a thing in this sentence: *I halve spellcheck, and it wood seam that these is all I really knead.* Yet there is almost nothing correct in that sentence! Students need to edit and rewrite as needed to develop and strengthen their writing.

The objective of editing is to use rigorous and relevant thinking to correct errors in grammar, spelling, and punctuation. Editing allows students to apply what they have learned about grammar, spelling, and punctuation to find and correct errors in their writing. These activities fit into Quadrant D on the Rigor/Relevance Framework.

Applying the Strategy

Editing is important for any writing assignment in middle school or high school. Students will find editing vital in all content areas:

- Science
  - fixing subject-verb agreement in a report on the invention that has had the greatest impact on the world

- Social Studies
  - correcting capitalization of place names in a brochure on the Seven Ancient Wonders of the World
- Math
  - checking spelling in an explanation of the difference between parallel and perpendicular lines
- ELA
  - correcting pronoun use in a short story about a lost pet — through the pet's point of view

Common Core State Standards

College and Career Readiness Anchor Standards for Writing

Text Types and Purposes

1. Write arguments to support claims in an analysis of substantive topics or texts, using valid reasoning and relevant and sufficient evidence.

Production and Distribution of Writing

4. Produce clear and coherent writing in which the development, organization, and style are appropriate to task, purpose, and audience.

5. Develop and strengthen writing as needed by planning, revising, editing, rewriting, or trying a new approach.

Range of Writing

10. Write routinely over extended time frames (time for research, reflection, and revision) and shorter time frames (a single sitting or a day or two) for a range of tasks, purposes, and audiences.

Teaching the Strategy

Introduce the strategy by explaining that the main purpose of editing is to correct errors in the following elements of writing to make a text stronger and clearer:

- Grammar
- Spelling
- Punctuation
- Capitalization

To edit written work, follow these steps:

1. Read the text silently and carefully, looking for errors.
2. Read the text aloud, listening to the sound of words and phrases.
3. Read the text a third time, moving a pencil, pen, or piece of paper under each line of text to be sure you look at every word.
4. Use a dictionary to check spelling.
5. Indicate changes with proofreading marks.

Grammar

Common errors in usage include the following:

1. **Subjects and verbs that disagree.** The basic rule states that a singular subject takes a singular verb, while a plural subject takes a plural verb. However, the number of the subject is not always clear, as the examples below show. To check subject-verb agreement, locate the subject of each sentence. Then be sure it agrees in number with the verb.

   Incorrect: The <u>children walks</u> to school.
   Correct: The <u>children walk</u> to school.

   Incorrect: <u>Neither Liz nor Shauna are</u> coming to the party.
   Correct: <u>Neither Liz nor Shauna is</u> coming to the party.

327

Incorrect: <u>My aunt and my uncle</u> <u>visits</u> us each year
Correct: <u>My aunt and my uncle</u> <u>visit</u> us each year.

Incorrect: <u>Each of the experiments</u> <u>are</u> done twice.
Correct: <u>Each of the experiments</u> <u>is</u> done twice.

Incorrect: He is one of the speakers <u>who</u> <u>is</u> scheduled.
Correct: He is one of the speakers <u>who</u> <u>are</u> scheduled.

2. **Pronouns and antecedents that disagree in number or gender.** An antecedent is the word to which a pronoun refers. The pronoun and its antecedent must agree in number. To check pronoun-antecedent agreement, find each pronoun in a sentence. Then locate its antecedent and be sure they agree.

Incorrect: The <u>boys</u> got ready for <u>his</u> game.
Correct: The <u>boys</u> got ready for <u>their</u> game.

Incorrect: <u>Paula</u> worried that <u>her</u> <u>sisters</u> would forget <u>her</u> lunches.
Correct: <u>Paula</u> worried that <u>her</u> <u>sisters</u> would forget <u>their</u> lunches.

Incorrect: <u>Everyone</u> prepared <u>their</u> favorite food.
Correct: <u>Everyone</u> prepared <u>his or her</u> favorite food.
Correct: All the <u>people</u> prepared <u>their</u> favorite food.

3. **Irregular verb misuse.** It's easy to misuse irregular verbs such as be, go, and have. This chart of irregular verb tenses can help. To check usage of irregular verbs, locate the verbs in the sentence and check the sentence tense. Be sure tenses are correct and consistent throughout the work.

	Be	**Go**	**Have**
Present	am, is, are	go, goes	have, has
Past	was, were	went	had
Future	will be	will go	will have

Spelling

Spellcheck programs can be useful to find misspelled words, but reading over a work carefully is important too. A spellcheck program won't catch homophones that are spelled correctly. Some commonly confused words can trip up the best spellers. Here's a list of commonly confused words.

- accept — to receive: *The winners <u>accept</u> the medals.*

- except — with the exception of: *Everyone went to the party <u>except</u> Willa.*

- affect — to influence: *The play <u>affected</u> me deeply.*

- effect —*n.*, result, *v.*, to accomplish: *The coffee had no <u>effect</u> on Paul.*

- all ready — prepared: *Jamal was <u>all ready</u> when his name was called.*

- already — by this time: *It was <u>already</u> too late to try out for the play.*

- altogether — entirely: *Theresa decided to try an <u>altogether</u> new approach to the essay.*

- all together — gathered, with everything in one place: *The class stood <u>all together</u> for the ceremony.*

- its — of or belonging to it: *The cat arched <u>its</u> back.*

- it's — contraction for it is: *We cannot tell if <u>it's</u> going to rain.*

- lie — to lie down: *The kindergarteners <u>lie</u> on their pallets.*

- lay — to lay an object down: *Saul will carefully <u>lay</u> his tools on the table.*

- passed — past tense of "to pass," to have moved: *We passed the ball around the circle.*

- past — belonging to a former time or place: *In the past, I lived near the beach.*

- than — use with comparisons: *Rita is a faster runner <u>than</u> Moira.*

- then — at that time, or next: *We can go swimming, and <u>then</u> we can have a barbeque.*

- their — possessive form of "they": *The actors took their bows.*

- there — indicates location: *William got there just in time.*

- they're — contraction for "they are": *They're going to the city for the weekend.*

- to — toward: *Lynn moved to the front of the line.*

- too — also, or excessively: *There was too much sauce on the pasta.*

- who — used as a subject or as a subject complement : *Who was in charge?*

- whom — used as an object: *To whom would you like to speak?*

Punctuation

As with grammar and spelling, editing for punctuation requires careful reading and checking. Common punctuation rules include the following:

1. Commas
   - Use commas to separate items written in a series such as words, phrases, subordinate clauses, and short independent clauses in a series.
   - Use a comma to separate two or more adjectives before a noun if the word order of the two could be reversed and the word "and" could be substituted for the comma.
   - Use commas to set off direct address.
   - Use commas to set off introductory words and expressions that interrupt the sentence.
   - Use commas to separate and enclose the separate items in dates and addresses.
   - Use a comma before *and, but,* and *or* in a compound sentence.
   - Use commas to set off and enclose an appositive (a word or phrase that can be substituted for a name).

- Use commas to set off and enclose nonessential phrases or clauses (e.g., participial phrases or dependent clauses which are not essential to the meaning of the sentence).

- Use a comma after an introductory clause or more than one phrase at the beginning of a sentence.

- Use a comma after the greeting in a friendly letter and after the closing expression.

2. Quotation marks

- Use quotation marks to indicate words directly quoted from another source, whether that source is a person or another work.

- Use quotation marks in pairs. Do not open a quotation and fail to close it at the end of the quoted material.

- Place commas and periods inside quotation marks. A comma usually precedes a direct quotation used within a sentence. Place colons and semicolons outside closed quotation marks. Place a question mark or exclamation point within closing quotation marks if the punctuation applies to the quotation itself. Place the punctuation outside the closing quotation marks if the punctuation applies to the whole sentence.

- Use single quotation marks to mark quotes within quotes.

3. Apostrophes

- Use an apostrophe to indicate possession.
  - Add 's to the singular form of the word, even if it ends in -s.
  - Add 's to the plural forms that do not end in -s.
  - Add ' to the end of plural nouns that end in -s.
  - Add 's to the end of compound words.
  - Add 's to the last noun to show joint possession of an object: or to show missing letters in contractions

- Use an apostrophe to indicate the missing letters in contractions.

Capitalization

Here are some common rules for capitalizing letters.

- Capitalize the first word of a sentence and the pronoun *I* in any location.
- Capitalize the first word in a quotation.
- Capitalize proper nouns and most adjectives derived from proper nouns.
- Capitalize the first word and all titles and nouns in the salutation of a letter and the first word in the complimentary close.
- Capitalize the names of the days of the week, holidays, months of the year, historic events, and eras.
- Capitalize the first, last, and all other important words in the titles of written works (documents, books, journals, newspapers, reports) and their contents (chapters, sections, articles), works of art and music, and movies. In titles, only capitalize prepositions or conjunctions when they are the first or last word in the title or subtitle.
- Capitalize the names of people and words associated with the name (places, diseases, etc.).
- Capitalize the specific names of geographical sites and places, regions, organizations, buildings, and state abbreviations.
- Capitalize words based on nationalities or historical background.

Directed Writing Activity

1. This activity will require students to develop and strengthen writing as needed by editing. They will edit the introduction they have revised.

2. Pass out the proofreading symbols form. Explain how each symbol is used to indicate corrections needed in the text.

3. Have students read over the introduction they worked on in the revising exercise once, silently. They can then read their introductions aloud, but quietly. Finally, they can read their introductions a line at a time. At each step, they should mark errors in grammar, spelling, punctuation, and capitalization with proofreading symbols.

4. With the class, go over the editorial introduction and edit it. Encourage students to point out errors in grammar, spelling, punctuation, and capitalization.

Proofreading Symbols Form

Delete and Insert

ℛ Delete, take (it) out

ℛ Delete and close up

ℐ# Delete extra space

\# Insert space

∧ Insert text

ℓ Correct letter

Punctuation
(Use caret to show location)

⊙ Insert period∧

⊙ Insert comma∧

⊙ Insert colon∧

⊙ Insert semicolon∧

⹂ ⹂ Insert quotation marks∧

ˇ ˇ Insert single quotes∧

ˇ Insert apostrophe∧

⑦ Insert question mark∧

① Insert exclamation point∧

= Insert hyphen∧

( ) Insert parentheses∧

— Insert dash∧

Paragraph and Position

⌐ Move to right ⌐

⊏ ⊏Move to left

⌐⊏ ⌐Center⊏

⊓ Move up

⊔ Move down

𝑓𝑙 Flush left

𝑓𝑟 Flush right

══ Align horizontally

‖ Align vertically

⌠ Break, start new line

¶ New paragraph

𝑛𝑜 ¶ No new paragraph

⌐ run on

𝑓𝑙𝑢𝑠ℎ ¶ ←No paragraph indentation

∿ Transpose letters words or

5. After students complete their editing, review and discuss the assignment. Encourage students to explain where and why they have corrected errors.

6. Assign the independent writing activity. Review the four objectives of editing: correcting grammar, correcting spelling, correcting punctuation, and correcting capitalization. Then ask students to edit their revised editorial to develop and strengthen writing as needed.

For the Student

Independent Writing Activity

Follow these directions to edit your editorial, developing and strengthening the writing as needed.

1. Look carefully at the sample edited editorial. Note how the proofreading symbols show the corrections that need to be made.

2. Read the body and conclusion of your editorial carefully. Read it again aloud, quietly. Then go over it line by line.

3. Use the proofreading symbols form to mark corrections with proofreading symbols during each reading.

Sample Edited Editorial

Littering is a huge problem in ~~y~~arborough. The roads
are covered with garbage. People toss fast-food
wrap~~P~~ers out car windows. ~~They toss soda cans~~. *and soda cans* They
also dump
~~toss~~ old tires and clothing. ~~It is necessary that~~
has to be
something ~~is~~ done. I believe our best option is
educating the public.

If people knew the ~~a~~ffects of littering on ~~the economy~~
~~and~~ the environment, they would be less likely to toss
their trash. The things they throw out hurt the land,
plants, and animals. Old tires and electronics ~~They~~ can
be toxic. ~~A~~nimals eat plastic refuse. *and* ~~They~~ get tangled
in it. (Many people don't know ~~this~~) *that* ~~however. In the~~
~~event that~~ *If* there (were)(more) information available
about the effects of littering ~~on the land and living~~
people
~~creatures, littering~~ would be less likely to ~~be done by~~
litter.
~~people.~~

We can also appeal to people's civic pride. People
like their towns to look ~~nice~~ clean. ~~Milltown looks much~~
~~nicer than our town.~~ It's not nice to see all that ~~grungy~~
junk along our roads and in our streams and
meadows. If people ~~was aware of~~ knew how others look at
our town, they might feel ashamed and embarrassed –
and they might be willing to work to ~~stop~~ fix the
problem. There is also the economic cost of littering. Our
town gets a lot of ~~it's~~ its income from tourists, and Tourists
don't want to look at litter. ~~It follows, then, that~~ Therefore, too much litter
~~has the ability to~~ can hurt people's incomes. The hotel, ~~and~~
motel, restaurant, and shop owners ~~will~~ would all benefit from
a program to stop litter ing. Letting ~~him~~ them know how much
litter costs ~~them in business~~ their businesses will make them more
willing to support the effort.

It is clear ~~to see~~ that educating the public ~~be~~ is the best
way to address the problem ~~of~~ littering in our town. It
would be impossible to catch all the people ~~doing the~~ who
littering. We need to get townspeople to police ~~the~~
~~problem – and to stop doing it when they are the~~ themselves.
~~problem.~~ An education program about littering will
help to take our town from disgusting to delightful.

Proofreading Symbols Form

Delete and Insert

✗ Delete, take (it) out

✗ Delete and close up

❡# Delete ❡# extra space

\# Insert#space

∧ Insert∧text

e Corre∧ct letter

Punctuation
(Use caret to show location)

⊙ Insert period∧

⊘ Insert comma∧

⊙ Insert colon∧

⊙ Insert semicolon∧

❝ ❝ Insert quotation marks∧

❝ ❝ Insert∧single quotes∧

❝ Insert apostrophe∧

⑦ Insert question mark∧

① Insert exclamation point∧

= Insert∧hyphen

( ) Insert∧parentheses∧

— Insert∧dash

Paragraph and Position

] Move to right]

[[Move to left

] [ ]Center[

⊓ Move up

⊔ Move down

fl Flush left

fr Flush right

═ Align horizontally

| | Align vertically

⌠ Break, start new line

¶ New paragraph

no ¶ No new paragraph

⌐ run on

flush ¶ ← No paragraph indentation

∪ Transpose letters words or

Writing Process: Revising

For the Teacher

Defining the Strategy

When students have finished a draft, they may think they're done. But as the writer Richard North Patterson said, "Writing is rewriting." When the draft is done, it's time to revise — to develop and strengthen writing as needed by planning, revising, editing, rewriting, or trying a new approach.

The objective of revising is to use rigorous and relevant thinking to make a previous draft clearer and more precise. Revising fits within Quadrants C and D on the Rigor/Relevance Framework, allowing learners to think in complex ways while evaluating their work.

Applying the Strategy

Revising is a vital part of the writing process in middle school or high school. Students will find revising helpful in all content areas:

- Science
  - adding transitions to make the organization clearer in a research paper comparing and contrasting African and Asian elephants

- Social Studies
  - using strong word choice to explain why the bubonic plague was so devastating in the fourteenth century
- Math
  - adding facts to strengthen a paper describing a survey of local businesses
- ELA
  - combining sentences to make a short story more vivid and exciting

Common Core State Standards

College and Career Readiness Anchor Standards for Writing

Text Types and Purposes

1. Write arguments to support claims in an analysis of substantive topics or texts, using valid reasoning and relevant and sufficient evidence.

Production and Distribution of Writing

4. Produce clear and coherent writing in which the development, organization, and style are appropriate to task, purpose, and audience.
5. Develop and strengthen writing as needed by planning, revising, editing, rewriting, or trying a new approach.

Range of Writing

10. Write routinely over extended time frames (time for research, reflection, and revision) and shorter time frames (a single sitting or a day or two) for a range of tasks, purposes, and audiences.

Teaching the Strategy

Introduce the strategy by explaining that the main purpose of revising is to improve the following elements of writing:

- **Content.** Students can revise to include all the facts and details they need to create a strong piece of writing.
- **Organization.** Students can revise to ensure that their writing is organized logically and clearly, with transitions that show how one idea leads to the next.
- **Style.** Students can revise to choose strong, vivid words; an appropriate tone; and smooth sentences.

Peer Feedback

Because students may have difficulty objectively judging and revising their own writing, peer editing can be a useful tool. In peer editing, students exchange work with a partner and offer revision suggestions. This feedback form may be helpful for students.

Peer Feedback Form

Title: _____

Writer: _____

Responder: _____

One effective part of your (writing/project) was _____

_____

Because _____

One question I have is _____

_____

As you revise, be sure to _____

_____

Revising Content

When revising content, students should read through their draft slowly, stopping at the end of each section to ask themselves these questions:

- Is the information accurate?
- Is the information complete? Have I left out any facts or ideas necessary for my audience and purpose?
- Are all my ideas explained fully and understandably?
- Are there any steps missing from instructions or descriptions of processes?
- Have I included any unnecessary information?

Strategies for Revising Content

- Correct any inaccurate facts or details.
- Add further details, explanations, and instructions necessary for the purpose and audience.
- Be sure each of your details supports the main idea of the paragraph.
- Delete any information that is unessential and unimportant to readers.

Revising Organization

When revising organization, students should read their draft carefully and ask themselves these questions.

- Have I included headings and subheadings where necessary?
- Are all the elements of my writing present and in the appropriate order?
- Have I included transitions so that each paragraph follows logically from the preceding one?

Common Transitions

consequently	on the contrary	before
clearly	of course	before long
furthermore	in general	finally
in addition	therefore	first, second, third
moreover	in conclusion	in the first place
because	in other words	in the meantime
also	specifically	later
however	after	meanwhile
on the other hand	afterwards	next
but	as soon as	soon
yet	at first	then
nevertheless	at last	

Strategies for Revising Organization

- Add transitions where necessary.
- Move or modify paragraphs so that the progression of ideas is logical.

Revising for Style

To check for style problems, students should ask themselves:

- Are my sentences overly wordy?
- Have I used passive rather than active construction?
- Are my verbs and adjectives weak?
- Do I include run-ons or short, choppy sentences?
- Is my tone appropriate for my audience and purpose?

Strategies for Revising Style

- Replace wordy construction with concise terms.

Correcting Wordiness

Use...	To Replace
because, since, or why	for the reason that due to the fact that on the grounds that
if	in the event that under circumstances in which
about	in reference to with regard to
must or should	it is necessary that it is important that
can	is able to has the ability to
may, might, can, could	it is possible that there is a chance that it could happen that the possibility exists for
before, when, as, after	prior to in anticipation of subsequent to following on at the same time as simultaneously with

- Replace passive construction with active construction.
  - **Passive:** The changes will be decided on by the city council.
  - **Active:** The city council will decide on the changes.

- Replace weak verbs and adverbs with stronger ones.
  - **Weak:** The audience clapped loudly.
  - **Stronger:** The audience applauded wildly.
- Correct or divide run-on sentences, and combine short, choppy sentences.
  - **Run-on:** Elephants are at risk because the ivory in their tusks is very valuable and poachers hunt them for the ivory which they then sell at a huge profit, they cannot make as much from other activities.
  - **Corrected:** Elephants are at risk because the ivory in their tusks is very valuable. Poachers hunt them for the ivory, which they then sell at a huge profit. They cannot make as much from other activities.
  - **Short, choppy sentences:** Tamara cried out in fear. She saw a strange figure approaching. The figure was ghostly.
  - **Corrected:** Tamara cried out in fear when she saw a strange, ghostly figure approaching.
- Be sure that language — formal or informal — is appropriate for the audience and purpose.

Directed Writing Activity

1. This activity will require students to develop and strengthen writing as needed by revising, editing, rewriting, or trying a new approach. They will revise the introduction they have drafted.

2. Have students work with partners to look back at the introductions they wrote for the drafting activity.

3. Pass out the revising checklist and the peer feedback form. Have students read over their partner's introductions carefully.

4. Ask students to fill out the peer feedback form for the partner's introductions. Then students can revise their introductions for content, organization, and style.

5. With the class, discuss and revise the class introduction for an editorial. Encourage students to contribute ideas for revision.

6. After learners complete their revisions, review and discuss the assignment. Encourage students to read their work aloud and talk about whether the introductions introduce a claim and organize the reasons and evidence clearly.

7. Assign the independent writing activity. Review the three objectives of revision: revising for content, revising for organization, and revising for style. Then ask students to revise the draft of the editorial to develop and strengthen writing as needed.

Revision Checklist

Content

- ☐ Is the information accurate?
- ☐ Is the information complete? Have I left out any facts or ideas necessary for my audience and purpose?
- ☐ Are all my ideas explained fully and understandably?
- ☐ Are there any steps missing from instructions or descriptions of processes?
- ☐ Do I need to delete any unnecessary information?

Organization

- ☐ Have I included headings and subheadings where necessary?
- ☐ Are all the elements of my writing present and in the appropriate order?
- ☐ Have I included transitions so each paragraph follows logically from the preceding one?

Style

- ☐ Are my sentences wordy?
- ☐ Do I need to correct any passive voice constructions?
- ☐ Are there any weak verbs and adjectives?
- ☐ Do I need to divide run-on sentences or combine short, choppy sentences?
- ☐ Is my tone appropriate for my audience and purpose?

Sample Peer Feedback Form

Title: A Plea for Bicycle Lanes

Writer: Maria Gomez

Responder: Jenn Lalicki

One effective part of your (writing/project) was the examples you used showing how dangerous riding bikes without bike lanes can be

Because they had strong verbs and adjectives that showed what can happen without bike lanes

One question I have is how much it costs to put in bike lanes

As you revise, be sure to combine some of your short sentences and take out the slang

For the Student

Independent Writing Activity

Follow these directions to revise your editorial, developing and strengthening the writing as needed.

1. Look carefully at the sample revised editorial. Note how the changes correspond to the points on the checklist.

2. Have your partner look over the rest of the editorial you wrote for the drafting exercise and note suggestions made on the peer feedback form.

3. Use the Revising Checklist and Peer Feedback form to revise the editorial you wrote for the drafting exercise.

Sample Revised Editorial

Littering is a huge problem in Yarborough. The roads are covered with garbage. People toss fast-food wrappers, soda cans, old tires, and clothing out car windows. Something must be done. I believe our best option is educating the public.

If people knew the effects of littering on the economy and the environment, they would be less likely to toss their trash. The things they throw out hurt the land, plants, and animals. Many people don't know that old tires and electronics can be toxic, and animals eat and get tangled in plastic refuse. If there were more information available about the effects of littering, people would be less likely to litter.

We can also appeal to residents' civic pride. People like their towns to look nice. It's embarrassing to see all that junk along our roads and in our streams and meadows. If people were aware of how others look at our town, they might feel ashamed and embarrassed — and they might be willing to work to fix the problem.

In addition, there is the economic cost of littering. Our town gets a lot of its income from tourists, and tourists don't want to look at litter. This means that a town full of litter can hurt people's incomes. The hotel, motel, restaurant, and shop owners will all benefit from a program to stop litter. Letting them know how much litter costs them will make them more willing to support the effort.

Therefore, it is clear that educating the public is the best way to start addressing the problem of littering in our town. It would be impossible to catch and fine all the people who are littering, so we need to encourage townspeople to police themselves. An education program about littering will help to take our town from disgusting to delightful.

Revision Checklist

Content

- ☐ Is the information accurate?
- ☐ Is the information complete? Have I left out any facts or ideas necessary for my audience and purpose?
- ☐ Are all my ideas explained fully and understandably?
- ☐ Are there any steps missing from instructions or descriptions of processes?
- ☐ Do I need to delete any unnecessary information?

Organization

- ☐ Have I included headings and subheadings where necessary?
- ☐ Are all the elements of my writing present and in the appropriate order?
- ☐ Have I included transitions so each paragraph follows logically from the preceding one?

Style

- ☐ Are my sentences wordy?
- ☐ Do I need to correct any passive voice constructions?
- ☐ Are there any weak verbs and adjectives?
- ☐ Do I need to divide run-on sentences or combine short, choppy sentences?
- ☐ Is my tone appropriate for my audience and purpose?

Peer Feedback Form

Title: _____

Writer: _____

Responder: _____

One effective part of your (writing/project) was

_____

Because _____

One question I have is _____

_____

As you revise, be sure to _____

_____

Writing Process: Publishing/ Presenting

For the Teacher

Defining the Strategy

By this time, learners have finished prewriting, drafting, revising, and editing their text. *Done, at last!* they might think. But there is one more step to the writing process — publishing and presenting. This step can be the most exciting, and the most fun, for students. Putting their work in a public forum gives students the chance to produce and publish writing and to interact and collaborate with others.

The objective of publishing and presenting is to give work a real-world context. In any subject area, publishing requires students to adapt and apply their skills to unknown situations. This places publishing and presenting solidly within Quadrant D on the Rigor/Relevance Framework.

Applying the Strategy

Publishing and presenting is a useful end product in any writing assignment in middle school or high school. The skill can help students in these subject areas:

- Science
  - submitting an essay on a science project for a Young Naturalist Award
- Social Studies
  - creating a travel flyer giving historical information, statistics, and descriptions of a country's important tourist sites
- Math
  - creating a PowerPoint slide show for younger students that illustrates a complicated math concept
- ELA
  - submitting a poem to an online teen poetry magazine

Common Core State Standards

College and Career Readiness Anchor Standards for Writing

Text Types and Purposes

1. Write arguments to support claims in an analysis of substantive topics or texts, using valid reasoning and relevant and sufficient evidence.

Production and Distribution of Writing

6. Use technology, including the Internet, to produce and publish writing and to interact and collaborate with others.

Teaching the Strategy

Introduce the strategy by explaining that the main purposes of publishing and presenting are:

- To prepare a finished copy of a writing text that has gone through the prewriting, drafting, revising, and editing stages.
- To find or create an appropriate platform for the finished work that puts it in the public eye.

Preparing the Final Draft

Students who have taken a text through the writing process have made changes at several points:

- During revising, students have made changes in content, organization, and style.
- During editing, students have made changes in grammar, spelling, punctuation, and capitalization.

As they start the publishing process, students must go over their written work one last time and make a final, corrected copy. To do this, they should follow these steps.

1. Read over the revised and edited text carefully.
2. Be sure that details still support the thesis or main idea, or help to advance the plot and characterization.
3. Check to ensure that the organization is logical.
4. Double-check all editing changes.
5. Produce a final copy, incorporating all changes.
6. Read the final copy one last time, looking for errors.

A checklist can help students ensure that their final draft incorporates all the necessary changes and corrections.

Final Draft Checklist

☐	Do all my details support my thesis or advance my plot and characterization?
☐	Are my ideas organized logically, in a way that supports my purpose?
☐	Have I made all the necessary changes in content, organization, and style to ensure that my ideas are well-supported and flow from paragraph to paragraph?
☐	Have I made all the necessary changes in grammar, spelling, punctuation, and capitalization to ensure that my writing is free from errors?

Finding a Publishing/Presenting Platform

There are almost as many ways to publish or present a piece of writing as there are pieces of writing. Some of the possibilities include:

Platform	Type of Writing	Subject Area
PowerPoint	Instructions, directions	Any
Student newspaper	Article, editorial, short story, poetry	Social studies, science, ELA
Class blog	Essay, editorial, fiction, poetry	Any
Local newspaper	Article, letter to the editor	Social studies, science, ELA
Local writing competition	Essays, poetry, stories	Any
Computer publishing program	Brochures, flyers	Aocial studies, ELA
Online magazines/ newspaper sites	Essays, articles, stories, poetry	Any
Online writing competition	Essays, articles, stories, poetry	Any

The number of online sites devoted to student publication is huge and growing daily. Here are only some of the possible venues for student publishing and presenting. Check submission policies before sending in work.

Publication Name	URL	Type of Writing
The Apprentice Writer	http://www.susqu.edu/academics/10602.asp	Fiction, poetry, essays
Bookworm Magazine	http://www.bookworm-mag.com/	Fiction, poetry, essays, book reviews
The Claremont Review	http://www.theclaremontreview.ca/index.html	Poetry, fiction, drama
Cyberteens	http://www.cyberteens.com/index.html	Fiction, articles, poetry
Figment	http://figment.com/	Fiction, poetry
The Louisville Review	http://www.louisvillereview.org/	Poetry
Skipping Stones Magazine	http://www.skippingstones.org/index.html	Essays, stories, poetry, letters to the editor
Teen Ink	http://www.teenink.com/	Any
Spinebreakers	http://www.spinebreakers.co.uk/	Fiction, poetry
World of Reading	http://www.worldreading.org/	Book reviews
The Write Kids	http://writekids.tripod.com/index.htm	Articles, poetry
The Writer's Slate	http://www.writingconference.com/writer's.htm	Prose, poetry

There are also dozens of online contests where students compete to publish their work, too. It is important to check the contest deadline, of course, before submitting. Some possibilities include:

Contest Name	URL	Type of Writing
Courage in My Community Essay Contest	http://www.courageinmycommunity.com/default.html	Essays
Dupont Science Essay Challenge	http://thechallenge.dupont.com/	Science essays
Holocaust Remembrance Project Essay Contest	http://holocaust.hklaw.com/2012/index.asp	Essays
National Peace Essay Contest	http://www.usip.org/programs/initiatives/national-peace-essay-contest	Essays
Weekly Reader Student Publishing Contest	http://www.weeklyreader.com/spc	Nonfiction
The Writer's Conference	http://www.writingconference.com/writing.htm	Poetry, fiction, expository writing
Young Naturalist Award	http://www.amnh.org/nationalcenter/youngnaturalistawards/	Science essays
Young Playwrights Contest	http://www.youngplaywrights.org/National_Comp..html	Drama
Young Voices of America	http://www.youngvoicesfoundation.org/youngvoiceshome.html	Poetry, fiction, essays

A publishing/presenting options form can help students determine the most suitable publishing platforms for their work.

Publishing/Presenting Options Form

Platform	Why Suitable
1.	
2.	
3.	

Directed Writing Activity

1. This activity will require students to produce and publish writing and to interact and collaborate with others. Pass out the final draft checklist to students.

2. Go over the class editorial from the editing exercise. Discuss with students whether each point on the checklist has been achieved. Have a volunteer make a final copy of the editorial.

3. Review and discuss publication/presentation possibilities for the editorial. Ask students to suggest three possible publishing platforms and explain why they think the platforms would be suitable for the editorial.

4. Assign the independent writing activity.

Sample Revised Editorial

Littering is a huge problem in Yarborough. The roads are covered with garbage. People toss fast-food wrappers, soda cans, old tires, and clothing out car windows. Something must be done. I believe our best option is educating the public.

If people knew the effects of littering on the economy and the environment, they would be less likely to toss their trash. The things they throw out hurt the land, plants, and animals. Many people don't know that old tires and electronics can be toxic, and animals eat and get tangled in plastic refuse. If there were more information available about the effects of littering, people would be less likely to litter.

We can also appeal to residents' civic pride. People like their towns to look nice. It's embarrassing to see all that junk along our roads and in our streams and meadows. If people were aware of how others look at our town, they might feel ashamed and embarrassed — and they might be willing to work to fix the problem.

In addition, there is the economic cost of littering. Our town gets a lot of its income from tourists, and tourists don't want to look at litter. This means that a town full of litter can hurt people's incomes. The hotel, motel, restaurant, and shop owners will all benefit from a program to stop litter. Letting them know how much litter costs them will make them more willing to support the effort.

Therefore, it is clear that educating the public is the best way to start addressing the problem of littering in our town. It would be impossible to catch and fine all the people who are littering, so we need to encourage townspeople to police themselves. An education program about littering will help to take our town from disgusting to delightful.

Sample Publishing/Presenting Options Form

Platform	Why suitable
1. local newspaper	treats a topic of interest to local readers
2. class blog	topic has been part of class discussion
3. Teen Ink	fits the format and topic the online magazine requires

For the Student

Independent Writing Activity

Follow these directions to finalize and publish your editorial, using technology and the Internet, if appropriate, to produce and publish writing and to interact and collaborate with others.

1. Look carefully at the edited draft of your editorial.
2. Use the final draft checklist to ensure that you have made all the necessary changes and corrections in your editorial.
3. Make a clean final draft of your editorial.
4. Write two to three publishing/presenting possibilities for your editorial in the publishing/presenting options form.

Final Draft Checklist

☐ Do all my details support my thesis or advance my plot and characterization?

☐ Are my ideas organized logically, in a way that supports my purpose?

☐ Have I made all the necessary changes in content, organization, and style to ensure that my ideas are well-supported and flow from paragraph to paragraph?

☐ Have I made all the necessary changes in grammar, spelling, punctuation, and capitalization to ensure that my writing is free from errors?

Publishing/Presenting Options Form

Platform	Why Suitable
1.	
2.	
3.	